青年創業系列 ————

# 創業
# 法律指南  III

## Legal Guide
## for Business Starters

# 序言

## 熟知法律奠基礎，了解條文營商妥

「法律條例」往往予人一種艱澀難懂、刻板生硬、內容複雜棘手的印象，令人望而生畏。然而，對於年輕的創業家來說，掌握法律條文卻是不可或缺的技能。

例如在香港及大灣區城市成立公司，需要選擇合適的商業模式；聘請員工時，要熟知相關地區的僱傭條例和合約；推出新產品時，需要保護知識產權；公司逐漸壯大，要考慮籌集資金或進行風險融資；若與其他公司存在法律糾紛，需考慮採取法律行動來解決問題。這些都是青年創業家需要掌握的法律知識。

香港青年協會十分榮幸與孖士打律師行攜手合作編寫《創業法律指南III》，為有志於香港及大灣區創業的青年提供豐富的法律資訊，並總結初創公司常見的法律問題和陷阱，冀幫助他們解答疑難。

我們誠摯向有志創業的青年推薦此書，相信它將您提供實用的法律參考，助您在創業的路途上邁出成功的第一步。

何永昌先生，MH
香港青年協會總幹事

# 序言

過去 20 年以來，香港政府、非政府機構和商界逐漸提供更多的財政資源並製定孵化及導師計劃以支持青年在香港創業。香港青年協會推出的香港青年創業計劃便是眾多支持方式之一。作為青年企業者在創業過程中掌握法律框架的工具，香港青年協會於 2007 年和 2014 年先後兩次出版了《創業法律指南》。

本《法律指南》（現已出版到第三版）旨在，對我們的青年在現行法律框架下創業時一般可能遇見的法律問題提供一個全面的概述[1]。涵蓋的常見問題包括公司、僱傭、知識產權、融資及爭議解決等類別。考慮到香港企業有機會在大灣區拓展業務，這些問題也會在內地法律的框架下予以簡要闡述。

對法律的理解能為企業的良好治理、可持續及最終的成功奠定了基礎。本《法律指南》為剛起步的青年企業家、正在擴大規模的初創企業和為創業者提供支援服務的人員提供一個有用的資源。

本《法律指南》由孖士打律師行與香港青年協會通力協作編製。本出版書籍的內容僅為相關事項提供一般性指引，不構成法律意見，也不能替代針對個別情況出具的特定意見。讀者在參照本《法律指南》所討論的事項而採取有關的任何行動之前應尋求法律意見。

---

[1] 截至 2023 年 7 月 1 日。

董光顯

孖士打律師行 首席合夥人

# 目錄

002 — 003 | 序言

006 — 016 | 第一章　商業載體

017 — 026 | 第二章　僱傭

027 — 031 | 第三章　知識產權，即版權、商標、專利及註冊外觀設計

032 — 038 | 第四章　籌集資金的類型

039 — 047 | 第五章　通過天使投資人及眾籌開展社會化風險融資

048 — 053 | 第六章　爭議解決

054 | 香港青年協會簡介

055 — 057 | 香港青年協會社會創新及青年創業部簡介

058 — 060 | 孖士打律師行簡介

061 | 鳴謝

062 | 免責聲明

第一章 商業載體

## 概述

1. 初創企業的首要步驟之一是為其運營建立一個商業載體。 本章介紹香港常用的商業載體類型。

2. 在香港最常用的商業載體是私人股份有限公司。 這是本章的重點內容。

## 常用的商業載體類型

3. 商業載體的選擇取決於諸多因素，例如業務規模、管理結構、資金來源、風險承受力、靈活性等。 在香港最常用的商業載體類型為：

   ▌ 私人公司；

   ▌ 合夥；及

   ▌ 獨資經營。

4. 在內地最常用的商業載體類型與香港類似，儘管有些術語不同。

## ▌ 私人公司

5. 私人公司是獨立於其股東的法人實體。 這意味著每名股東的責任原則上僅限於該股東所持股份的未付金額（如有）。

6. 私人公司的股東人數上限為 50 人（不包括僱員和前僱員）。私人公司不得向公眾發出認購其任何股份的任何邀請。 對股東轉讓其在私人公司股份的權利是有限制的。

7. 在內地，最接近於私人公司的商業載體是有限責任公司（「有限責任公司」）。有限責任公司也是一個獨立的法律實體，每名股東的責任僅限於該股東認購的註冊資本金額。有限責任公司的股東人數上限也是 50 人。有限責任公司的股權可以在股東之間自由轉讓，但向第三方轉讓則受到限制。

## ▌ 合夥

8. 在香港，合夥可以採用普通合夥或有限責任合夥的形式。

9. 香港普通合夥不具備獨立的法人資格。 這意味著合夥人對合夥的債務承擔無限的個人責任；即合夥人的責任不受限於其對合夥的出資。

10. 內地普通合夥企業的主要特點與香港普通合夥相似。

11. 內地合夥企業還可採用特殊的普通合夥企業的形式，但是，該等形式的合夥僅可用於專業服務提供方，例如律師事務所和會計師事務所。

12. 有限責任合夥可以看作為私人有限公司與普通合夥的混合體。

13. 在香港，一家有限責任合夥須由一名或多名普通合夥人和一名或多名有限責任合夥人組成。普通合夥人負責管理合夥,並對合夥的債務承擔無限個人責任。有限責任合夥人不參與管理合夥,除了某些例外情況外,有限責任合夥人的責任僅限於其對合夥的出資額。

14. 內地有限合夥企業的主要特點與香港有限責任合夥相似。

## ▌ *獨資經營*

15. 香港獨資經營是由個人完全並直接擁有的非法團業務,不是一個獨立的法律實體。 這意味著個人對獨資經營的債務負有無限的個人責任。

16. 內地獨資經營的主要特點與香港獨資經營相似。

# 私人公司和有限責任公司

17. 私人公司和有限責任公司是在香港和內地最為常用的商業載體。本部分更為詳細地介紹私人公司和有限責任公司的以下方面:

(1) 成立;

(2) 股本;

(3) 公司治理; 及

(4) 主要通報及存檔的要求。

## ▌ *成立*

18. 在香港成立一家私人公司是一個相對簡單及快捷的程序。 私人公司的成立可以通過向公司註冊處提交下列文件申請:

(1) 填妥的法團成立表格（其中包含有關私人公司的董事、秘書、股東、股本等具體信息）；

(2) 其組織章程細則；

(3) 致商業登記署通知書（是一項商業登記申請）；及

(4) 規定的費用及徵費。

19. 在取得成立申請的批准後，公司註冊處會簽發證明公司成立日期的公司註冊證明書，而稅務局會簽發商業登記證。

20. 批准程序約需四個工作日完成。

21. 相比之下，在內地設立一家有限責任公司的程序略為複雜及費時。有限責任公司的設立可以通過向國家市場監管總局（「市場監管局」）的地方機構提交以下申請材料：

(1) 申請表；

(2) 股東資格文件及自然人股東身份證明；

(3) 關於居住地或主要營業地的文件；

(4) 有限責任公司的章程；及

(5) 任何法律或行政法規或市場監管局要求提交的其他材料。

22. 在批准公司設立登記申請後，市場監管局的地方機構會向有限責任公司簽發營業執照。營業執照的簽發日期為有限責任公司的成立日期。設立程序的審批時間因申請人的身份而有所不同。如果申請人是內地居民，設立程序通常需要一至兩週完成。如果申請人是香港居民，則在內地設立有限責任公司將被視為外商獨資企業，而設立程序可能需要數月完成。

## ▍ 股本

23. 除非私人公司或有限責任公司屬於受規管的行業（例如銀行業或保險業），否則對最低或最高股本並無要求。

24. 私人公司可以通過發行股份獲取現金或非現金資產（例如房產）。有限責任公司的情況與之相似。

25. 在香港，股本可以劃分為不同類別的股份，且該等股份附帶私人公司組織章程細則所規定的特殊權利，但對於內地有限責任公司而言，情況則有些不確定。

## ▍ 公司治理

<u>董事</u>

26. 管理私人公司的一般權力通常歸屬於其董事。

27. 私人公司需任命至少一名自然人董事。對董事人數的上限沒有法律要求。董事可以是任何國籍、住所及居住地的個人 (18歲以上 ) 或法團。[2]

28. 董事對私人公司的責任源自多個方面，包括《公司條例》（第622章 )(《公司條例》)、相關判例及私人公司的組織章程細則。董事責任的概括性原則如下所列：

   (1) 有責任真誠地以私人公司的利益為前提行事；

   (2) 有責任為適當目的使用權力；

(3) 有責任不轉授權力 ( 經正式授權者除外 ) 並有責任作出獨立判斷；

(4) 有責任以合理的謹慎、技能及勤勉行事；

(5) 有責任避免個人利益與公司利益發生衝突；

(6) 有責任不進行有利益關係的交易 ( 但符合法律規定的情況除外 )；

(7) 有責任不利用董事職位謀取利益；

(8) 負有保密責任並有責任不將公司的資料作未經授權的用途；

(9) 有責任不接受第三方因該董事的職位而給予該董事的個人利益；

(10) 有責任遵守私人公司的章程 ( 包括其組織章程細則 ) 及決議；及

(11) 保存妥善帳簿的責任。

29. 有限責任公司需委任至少一名執行董事。 董事對有限責任公司的責任源自多個方面，包括《中華人民共和國公司法》(《中國公司法》)、相關行政法規及有限責任公司的章程。 有限責任公司董事責任的概括性原則與適用於私人公司董事責任的概括性原則相似。

<u>股東</u>

30. 私人公司需至少有一名註冊股東，其姓名、地址及持股情況應在公司註冊處公共記錄中存檔。 股東可以是個人或法團。

31. 股東管理私人公司的一般權力受限於《公司條例》的規定、相關判例法所規定的情況及私人公司的組織章程細則。 例如，《公司條例》要求諸如以下事項須經股東批准：

   (1) 變更組織章程細則；

   (2) 減少股本；

   (3) 任命及罷免審計師； 及

   (4) 任命及罷免董事。

32. 類似於私人公司，有限責任公司需至少有一名股東。 但是，有限責任公司通常會有兩名或兩名以上的股東，因為額外的規則會適用於僅有一名股東的有限責任公司。 例如，如果唯一股東不能證明有限責任公司的資產與唯一股東的資產完全分開，且不干涉諸如有限責任公司的資金，則唯一股東對該有限責任公司的債務承擔連帶責任。

33. 股東管理有限責任公司的一般權力受限於《中國公司法》的規定及有限責任公司的章程。《中國公司法》要求須經股東批准的事項類別與《公司條例》所規定的類別相似。

公司秘書

34. 私人公司需有一名公司秘書，該公司秘書可以是註冊辦事處或營業地點在香港的另一家公司，或者是通常居住在香港的個人。

35. 如果私人公司僅有一名董事，則公司秘書不能是其唯一董事，或當公司秘書是法人團體時，則公司秘書的唯一董事也不能是該私人公司的唯一董事。

36. 公司秘書的職能是保存私人公司的法定簿冊，包括董事及股東登記冊、董事會及股東會的會議記錄簿及股份證明書簿冊,以及準備須在公共記錄中存檔的文件。

37. 但是,內地對有限責任公司任命公司秘書並無強制性要求。

## 法定代表人

38. 「法定代表人」是《中國公司法》下的一個概念,在《公司條例》下並不存在。 有限責任公司須任命一名法定代表人。 法定代表人是有限責任公司的首要代表,擁有代表及約束有限責任公司的法定權力。

39. 有限責任公司的法定代表人僅可由有限責任公司的董事長、執行董事或經理擔任。

## 監事

40. 「監事」是《中國公司法》下的一個概念,在《公司條例》下並不存在。 有限責任公司需委任至少一名監事。 監事的職能是監督有限責任公司的董事和高級管理人員。 因此,監事不得由有限責任公司的董事或高級管理人員擔任。本部分以下列出了一些主要的通報及存檔要求。

## ■ 主要的通報及存檔要求

41. 私人公司需按照《公司條例》遵守特定的通報及存檔義務。 同樣地,有限責任公司需按照《中國公司法》遵守特定的報告及備案義務。本部份以下列出了一些主要的通報及存檔要求。

## 財務報表

42. 私人公司需保存妥當的帳簿。 其帳目須每年進行審計。 經審計的財務報表須提交給香港稅務局,並在股東周年大會上呈遞給股東。

43. 類似地，有限責任公司需保存妥當並經每年審計的帳簿。 經審計的財務報表須在其章程規定的時限內提交給股東。

簿冊及登記冊

44. 私人公司需保存特定的簿冊及登記冊，例如：

(1) 股東登記冊，記錄自公司成立以來公司每名股東及其各自持股比例的詳情；

(2) 董事登記冊，記錄自公司成立以來公司每名董事的詳情；

(3) 公司秘書登記冊，記錄自公司成立以來公司每名秘書的詳情；

(4) 押記登記冊，記錄影響公司財產或經營的每項押記的詳情；

(5) 一套所有董事會會議及股東會會議的會議記錄簿，包括公司董事和股東通過的所有決議； 及

(6) 重要控制人登記冊，記錄公司每名重要控制人的詳情 (定義見《公司條例》)。

45. 在內地，有限責任公司需在市場監管局保存股東登記冊及有關所有股東姓名或名稱的記錄。

周年申報表及變更通知

46. 私人公司需每年向公司註冊處提交周年申報表。 周年申報表顯示有關公司股本、股東、董事及已登記押記的最新詳情。

47. 此外，在發生諸如以下所述的變更後並在規定的期限內，私人公司需通知公司註冊處而有限責任公司需通知市場監管局：

(1) 公司名稱的任何變更；

(2) 組織章程細則或章程的任何變更；

(3) 董事或公司秘書的任何變更（或任何現有董事或公司秘書已存檔詳情的任何變更）；

(4) 註冊辦事處地址的任何變更； 及

(5) 任何股份配發。

## 股東協議

48. 股東協議是規管公司事務的重要法律文件。

49. 股東協議的主要目的是：

(1) 從即將進入籌資階段的初創企業創始人的角度而言，規定創始人和投資人相互之間的責任及義務； 及

(2) 從希望投資初創企業的投資人的角度而言，通過股東協議的條款確保業務的穩定性。

### 董事會代表

50. 通常而言，投資人希望擁有某種形式的董事會代表，以便其能夠對公司的經營擁有發言權。

51. 另一方面，創始人也希望確保其對董事會保持足夠的控制。 因此，股東協議可以賦權創始人任命及罷免董事會董事，且賦權持有一定比例股份的投資人任命董事。

52. 就某些決議而言，投資人可以要求公司的某些決定在作為決議通過之前需取得所有股東的一致同意，例如配發股份、變更公司資本結構及修改公司章程。

53. 該機制使投資人作為小股東能夠在公司的重大決策上擁有發言權。

54. 從創始人的角度而言，其應注意考慮保留事項的條款是否會妨礙創始人對公司日常運作迅速做出決定的能力。

### 對股份轉讓的限制

55. 從創始人的角度而言，股東協議應包含對股份轉讓的限制。 最常見的限制類型是優先購買權，根據該限制，股東如果希望向第三方出售股份，須先按照相同的條款及條件向其他股東提出要約出售該等股份。 如果要約未被接受，股東才可將股份出售給第三方。

### 拖售權

56. 這項權利確保在創始人決定出售初創企業時，其能夠促使所有其他股東也將持有的股份出售給同一位第三方買家。

57. 從創始人的角度而言，這項權利通過消除難纏的小股東阻撓出售初創企業的風險，提供了靈活性及便捷的退出途徑。

58. 從投資人的角度而言，該項權利確保其在退出過程中受到同等對待。

---

[2] 如果私人公司是上市公司所屬公司集團的成員，則不允許設立公司董事。

## 概述

1. 與內地 ( 包括大灣區 )、歐盟和美國等許多其他司法管轄區相比，香港對僱傭的規管較寬鬆。主要的法例即《僱傭條例》，規定了大部分僱員的某些基本權利及保障，且除少數例外情況外，同等地適用於在香港根據僱傭合同受僱的所有僱員。

2. 一般而言，僱傭合同約定僱主與僱員之間的關係。僱傭合同中試圖削減《僱傭條例》所賦予僱員任何權利、利益或保障的任何條款或條件均屬無效。因此，在任何合同條款不利的情況下，應以《僱傭條例》為準。

3. 在內地，與僱傭相關的主要法律是《中華人民共和國勞動法》及《中華人民共和國勞動合同法》(《勞動合同法》)。此外，還有與勞動爭議的調解與仲裁、社會保險費、勞務派遣等方面有關的專門法律 ( 且在某些情形下，還有特定城市的法規 )。

## 工作權[3]

4. 僱主須確保其僱員有權在香港工作。一般而言，除非擁有香港特區的居留權或入境權，任何人士均應取得適當的簽證才能在香港工作。僱主通常是就業簽證的保證人，在僱員的香港許可逗留期屆滿時需負責該僱員的遣返。

5. 香港居民在內地工作無需申請工作許可證，可以使用其港澳台居民居住證或港澳居民來往內地通行證作為有效的身份證件。對於沒有港澳台居民居住證或港澳居民來往內地通行證的人士，須辦理工作簽證 (Z 簽證 ) 及居留許可。

## 獨立承包商與僱員的區分

6. 確定一名工作人員是僱員還是獨立承包商是很重要的，因為獨立承包商不能同樣地獲得諸如《僱傭條例》所規定僱員能享有的福利及保護。現代的方法是對照一系列因素審查雙方關係的所有特徵，然後以一個整體印象來決定該等關係是否一種僱傭關係 ( 雙方對該等關係的稱謂並不是決定性的，往往不是考慮因素之一 )。

7. 法院考慮的因素包括諸如 ( 這不是一份窮盡的清單，每個因素的重要性取決於具體情形 ): 僱主對個人的控制程度、僱主提供工作的義務和個人接受工作的義務、個人是否須自行安排工具及設備等。

## 僱員享有的福利及待遇

### ▌ 合同形式 [4]

8. 與內地不同，香港不要求僱傭合同須是書面形式。但是，在僱傭開始前，僱員提出書面要求後，僱主須提供某些僱傭條件的書面詳情。如果僱傭合同是書面形式的，僱主須在簽署後立即向僱員提供一份副本。需要說明的基本條件是工資及發薪周期、年終酬金的款額 ( 如有 ) 或按比例應得的年終酬金及終止僱傭關係所需的通知期。

9. 在內地，勞動合同（相當於香港的僱傭合同）須由雙方以書面形式簽署（某些兼職僱員除外），如果不遵守，僱主會受到處罰。前段提及的基本條件可以納入勞動合同本身，也可以通過勞動合同援引員工手冊的方式將其納入。

## ▎*工資*[5]

10. 除某些例外情況外，僱主須向僱員支付法定最低工資。自2023年5月1日起，法定最低工資水平已提高至每小時40港元。

11. 在內地，最低工資水平因城市而異，且全職僱員與兼職僱員的最低工資水平也可能因城市而有所不同。

## ▎*工時*[6]

12. 除了有關工業企業僱傭青年人適用專門法規外，沒有任何法定條文規定最高工作時數。但《僱傭條例》規定，除帶薪法定（公眾）假日外，僱員有權在每7日內享有不少於一天的休息日。

13. 在內地，僱員的標準工時不應超過每日8小時、每周44小時，並且每周應至少有一個休息日（即分別為「標準工時制」）。加班工資應在標準工時制之外，根據額外工時是在工作日、休息日還是法定假日，分別按150%、200% 及300% 支付。經有關勞動部門批准，僱員也可以按「不定時工時制」或「綜合計算工時制」工作。

## ▎*年假*[7]

14. 僱員每受僱12個月有權享有最少7至14天的年假，具體天數基於服務年限計算。

15. 在內地，連續工作12個月（在任何僱主處）的僱員有權在每個日曆年享有最少5至15天的年假，具體天數也是基於在任何僱主處（無論是當前還是以前的僱主）工作的累計工齡計算。

## ▌ 病假[8]

16. 僱員有權享有帶薪病假，按照其日平均工資五分之四的比率計算。有權享有的病假可以按在最初受僱的12個月內每連續受僱滿一個月享有2個帶薪病假日的比率累積，此後每個月按4個帶薪病假日的比率累積，最多可以累積120個帶薪病假日。但是，除與生育有關的疾病外，疾病津貼僅適用於因疾病超過連續4天的缺勤。

17. 在內地，僱員的病假權利取決於疾病或受傷是否與工作有關。就與工作有關的疾病或受傷，僱員通常有權獲得最長12個月的全薪病假，但須出示必要的醫療證明。就與工作無關的疾病或受傷，法律沒有規定病假的最長天數，但僱員有權就疾病或受傷享有「醫療期」，期限為3至24個月，具體期限取決於僱員的服務年限（在任何僱主處）。在醫療期內的工資款額不得低於適用的最低工資的80%（雖然該比例在不同城市可能不同），且僱主在該期間不能單方面終止與僱員的僱傭關係。

## ▌ 產假及陪產假[9]

18. 在符合《僱傭條例》下特定資格要求的前提下，女性僱員有權享有14周的帶薪產假（自2020年12月11日起從10周增加到14周），或依照僱傭條款的約定執行，以更有利者為準。產假薪酬按僱員的日平均工資五分之四的比率支付。就2020年修訂案增加的4周，香港政府將向僱主報銷增加的產假薪酬，上限為80,000港元。

19. 在符合《僱傭條例》下特定資格要求的前提下，男性僱員有權按其日平均工資五分之四的比率，就其配偶／伴侶的每次分娩享有5個工作日的帶薪陪產假。

20. 在內地，女性僱員有權就其第一個子女享有總共98天的產假，包括在預產期前的15天產假。如果僱員難產或一次分娩一個以上子女，可以額外獲得15天的產假。不同的地方規定對產假的規定可能不同。在女性僱員休產假期間，僱主須向其支付不低於其正常工資的薪酬。

21. 此外，男性僱員有權享有7至30天的陪產假，具體天數取決於內地的當地地方性規定，但前提是該僱員的妻子生育的是第一個子女。在男性僱員休陪產假期間，僱主須向其支付不低於其正常工資的薪酬。

## ▌ 強制性公積金、退休及社會保險計劃 [10]

22. 香港的每個僱主均需向已註冊為強制性公積金計劃的退休計劃供款，金額至少為僱員月薪的5%（上限為1,500港元）。每位僱員也需向該計劃繳納至少為其月薪的5%（上限也為1,500港元）。但是，這個一般規則也有一些例外情況。

23. 在內地，僱主及僱員均需按月繳納由基本養老保險、基本醫療保險、失業保險、工傷保險、生育保險及住房公積金組成的基本社會保險。僱主與僱員的繳款總額按照勞動關係所在城市的規定，一般為僱員月工資的一個百分比。僱主與僱員的繳款總額按照該僱員月工資的一個特定百分比執行（其中僱主的繳款額一般高於僱員的繳款額，但均設有一個上限，即前一年當地平均月工資的三倍）。

## ▌ 僱員補償 [11]

24. 僱主須投保工傷相關保險，但除此之外，沒有提供醫療福利的法定要求。

25. 除上文第23段所述的社會保險外，內地沒有額外的強制性保險。

## ▌ *遣散費及長期服務金* [12]

26. 已連續受僱不少於24個月的僱員，如果其因裁減人員而遭解僱或該僱員遭停工，則其有權獲得法定的遣散費。已受僱於連續合同不少於5年的僱員在僱傭終止時可以獲得長期服務金（因不當行為遭立即解僱的除外）。

27. 獲取遣散費的權利與獲取長期服務金的權利只能二擇其一。每受僱一年，遣散費／長期服務金的款額為月薪的三分之二或22,500港元的三分之二（即15,000港元），以較低者為準，並以390,000港元封頂。涵蓋同一期限基於服務年限的任何合約性酬金可以從應向僱員支付的遣散費／長期服務金中扣除。此外，僱主擁有法定權利通過對沖的方式將某僱員已繳納的強制性公積金或退休計劃的款項減少其應向該僱員支付的遣散費或長期服務金（但該對沖機制將於2025年5月1日起廢除，屆時僱主的強制性公積金繳款所產生的福利不能再用於對沖應向僱員支付的遣散費或長期服務金）。

28. 在內地，遣散費被稱為「法定經濟補償」。在以下情況下，僱主一般需就終止勞動關係支付經濟補償：

(1) 僱主提議終止得到僱員的同意（即由僱主發起經雙方協商一致的終止）；

(2) 僱主單方面終止勞動關係（除非終止是基於《勞動合同法》第39條所列理由之一，例如僱員的嚴重不當行為 – 見下文「終止」）；

(3) 僱員因僱主未能遵守《勞動合同法》第38條所列的特定重要義務（例如未支付報酬（見下文「終止」））而辭職；

(4) 勞動關係在固定期限勞動合同期滿時終止（除非僱員拒絕了按前一份固定期限勞動合同所載的類似或更高條件續約的提議）；

(5) 因僱主破產、僱主的營業執照被吊銷，或僱主被責令關閉 / 註銷或選擇自願清算而終止僱傭。

## ▌ *終止* [13]

29. 僱主或僱員可以通過通知或支付代通知金的方式終止僱傭合同。作為代通知金支付的工資須按照《僱傭條例》計算。在特殊情況下，僱主可以基於《僱傭條例》第 9 條列明的任何法定理由（例如僱員作出欺詐或不忠實行為）立即解僱僱員（無需通知或支付代通知金）。

30. 試用期內的僱員，在試用期的第一個月內可以不經通知被終止僱傭，在試用期的第一個月後可以經不少於提前 7 天的通知被終止僱傭。試用期結束後或在沒有試用期的情況下，除被立即解僱的情況外，僱員有權享有與僱主在僱傭合同中約定的通知期，但不得少於 7 天。年假及產假不計入通知期。

31. 在僱員正在休病假並領取法定疾病津貼、懷孕、在勞工處簽發某些證書之前有權獲得法定僱員補償等情況下，終止聘用該僱員即屬違法。由於任何非法的歧視性原因而終止僱員的僱傭也屬違法（見下文）。

32. 在內地，勞動合同有兩種常見的類型：

(1) 固定期限勞動合同（涵蓋僱主與僱員商定的期限）；及

(2) 無固定期限勞動合同（規定無固定的期限）。

33. 在下列情況下，僱主需與僱員簽訂無固定期限合同：

(1) 在沒有書面合同的情況下僱員已為僱主工作一年；

(2) 僱員已完成與僱主訂立的前兩個固定期限合同；或

(3) 已為僱主工作10年或以上的僱員提出請求。

34. 勞動合同可以通過以下方式終止：

(1) 根據《勞動合同法》第36條的規定由雙方協商一致終止；

(2) 根據《勞動合同法》第37條的規定由僱員經提前30天發出通知（或在試用期內提前3天發出通知）或支付代通知金終止；

(3) 根據《勞動合同法》第38條的規定，僱主未能履行特定重要義務（例如未支付報酬），由僱員立即終止；

(4) 基於《勞動合同法》第39條規定的任何法定理由，例如僱員嚴重違反僱主的規章制度，由僱主立即終止；

(5) 基於《勞動合同法》第40條規定的任何無過錯理由（例如僱員不能勝任其工作，且經過培訓後仍不能勝任其工作），僱主提前30天發出通知（或在試用期內提前3天發出通知）或支付代通知金終止；或

(6) 根據《勞動合同法》第41條的規定，僱主因裁減人員終止。

## ▊ *反對違法歧視及騷擾的權利* [14]

35. 目前，香港的反歧視條例禁止基於性別、懷孕、母乳喂養、婚姻狀況、殘疾、家庭狀況及種族的歧視。香港沒有針對基於年齡或性取向歧視的保障措施，也沒有任何同酬的立法。

36. 在以下情形，僱主以禁止的原因歧視僱員，即屬違法：

(1) 該僱主以該等禁止的原因向該僱員提供可獲擢升、調職或訓練的機會，或任何其他利益、服務或設施；

(2) 藉該等禁止的原因拒絕讓該僱員或故意不讓該僱員獲得根據僱傭條款僱主提供給該僱員的該等機會或任何其他利益、服務或設施；或

(3) 以該等禁止的原因解僱該僱員或使該僱員遭受任何其他損害或不受歡迎的行為。

37. 香港的反歧視條例也禁止基於性別、母乳喂養、殘疾及種族的騷擾。違法騷擾指任何人以其中一個禁止的原因對另一人作出不受歡迎的行為。該等行為可能通過不同的形式進行，例如發表不恰當或冒犯性的言論或藉此作為笑話，且該等行為可能是一次性或重複性的行動。

38. 在內地，此話題仍是一個發展中的法律領域，但原則上禁止基於國籍、種族、性別、宗教信仰、殘疾、居住身份（即農村或城市僱員）或身體狀況（例如乙型肝炎等傳染性病原體的攜帶者）的歧視。新頒布的《中華人民共和國民法典》也明確禁止性騷擾，並建立了追究違法者責任的民事責任框架。因此，僱主須防止女性僱員在工作場所受到性騷擾（包括提供培訓及採取合理措施調查性騷擾投訴）。

## 僱主的納稅義務 [15]

39. 一般而言,香港的僱主有義務保存僱員的薪酬表記錄,並向香港稅務局通報僱員具體信息的任何變更。如果僱主收到僱主報稅表 (BIR56A),僱主須在一個月內填寫完畢並向香港稅務局提交。

40. 香港的僱主無需為僱員預扣稅款。但是,如果僱員打算在停止受僱後離開香港超過一個月,僱主需通知香港稅務局有關僱員即將離港,並須暫時保留所有應付僱員的款項,直至通知之日起一個月或收到香港稅務局發出的《同意釋款書》為止,以較早者為準。

41. 在內地,某些稅務申報的義務由僱主與僱員共同承擔。一般而言,僱主須按照《中華人民共和國個人所得稅法》從應付僱員的收入中預扣個人所得稅,但僱主未能按此行事並不免除僱員的納稅義務。

---

3　《入境條例》(第115章)
4　《僱傭條例》(第57章);《中華人民共和國勞動合同法》
5　《最低工資條例》(第608章);《中華人民共和國勞動法》;《中華人民共和國勞動合同法》
6　《僱傭條例》(第57章);《中華人民共和國勞動法》
7　《僱傭條例》(第57章);《中華人民共和國勞動法》;中國《職工帶薪年休假條例》
8　《僱傭條例》(第57章);中國《工傷保險條例》(2010年修訂);《中華人民共和國勞動法》;中國《企業職工患病或非因工負傷醫療期規定》(1994年);中國《關於貫徹執行<中華人民共和國勞動法>若干問題的意見》
9　《僱傭條例》(第57章);中國《女職工勞動保護特別規定》;《中華人民共和國勞動法》
10　《強制性公積金計劃條例》(第485章);《中華人民共和國社會保險法》
11　《僱員補償條例》(第282章);中國《工傷保險條例》
12　《僱傭條例》(第57章);《2022年僱傭及退休計劃法例(抵銷安排)(修訂)條例草案》;《中華人民共和國勞動法》;《中華人民共和國勞動合同法》
13　《僱傭條例》(第57章);《僱員補償條例》(第282章);《中華人民共和國勞動合同法》
14　《僱傭條例》(第57章);《性別歧視條例》(第480章);《殘疾歧視條例》(第487章);《家庭崗位歧視條例》(第527章);《種族歧視條例》(第602章);《中華人民共和國勞動法》;《中華人民共和國就業促進法》;中國《女職工勞動保護特別規定》;《中華人民共和國民法典》
15　《稅務條例》(第112章);《中華人民共和國個人所得稅法》(2018年修訂)

# 第三章 知識產權

### 即版權、商標、專利及註冊外觀設計

## 概述

1. 作品和發明可以受不同類別知識產權的保護，即版權、商標、專利和註冊外觀設計。

2. 知識產權具有地域性，可能需要也可能不需要註冊。 對於需要註冊的知識產權，應認真起草申請文件 ( 特別是專利 ) 並聘請律師指導整個申請過程。

3. 在香港註冊的知識產權不會自動在內地受到保護，反之亦然。 為了在香港、內地和任何其他司法管轄區獲得保護，須在每個司法管轄區分別進行註冊。 經營者應優先在其最重要的市場、研發地點及製造地點 ( 如有 ) 進行註冊。

4. 任何人在商品或服務中或為其業務複製或使用他人的知識產權均可能構成侵權。 侵權可能引起民事責任，甚至刑事責任。

# 知識產權的類別

## ▍ *版權*[16]

5. 版權保護特定類別的作品 ( 例如文學作品、戲劇作品、音樂作品、藝術作品、錄音製品、電影、廣播、有線電視節目和已出版版本的排版 ) 中對思想的表達 ( 但不是思想本身 )。 一件作品可以受一種或以上類別的版權保護。

6. 在香港和內地,如果作品是原創並以實物形式記錄下來,版權便會自動產生。 一件作品如果源自作者,並且是作者的技能、勞動和努力的結果,則視為「原創」。

7. 一般而言,作者是作品的第一版權人。 由僱員或獨立承包商受託創作的作品,即委託作品,適用以下特殊規則:

    (1) 在香港,僱員在其正常工作職責範圍內創作的作品,其版權屬於僱主,除非另有相反的協議。 在內地的情況則有所不同,除非另有相反的協議,僱員一般擁有作品的版權,但僱主擁有一定的權利享有該作品。

    (2) 根據香港和中國內地的法律,委託作品的版權歸屬取決於與獨立承包商簽署的協議。 如果沒有協議,或協議沒有相關規定,版權將默認屬於作為作者的獨立承包商。

8. 香港沒有版權註冊制度。 但是,版權註冊在內地是可選並建議進行的,因為在出現爭議時,可以作為所有權的表面證據。

9. 一般而言,版權的有效期為作者的剩餘壽命加上50年,但不同的保護期限可能適用於不同類別的版權作品。

## ▌ *商標*[17]

10. 商標是任何能夠將商品或服務與某一特定經營者聯繫起來的標誌（例如，文字或標識或兩者的組合）。 對已註冊商標，其所有權人可以根據成文法就侵權行為享受更有力的保護。 另外，未註冊的商標仍可以受普通法假冒行為的保護。

11. 申請註冊的商標須具有顯著特徵和非描述性，不得與在相關地區在先註冊的商標相同或混淆性相似。 註冊申請應涵蓋目前提供的和近期可能提供的商品和服務。

12. 註冊商標的有效期為10年，自核准註冊之日起計算，可以連續續展。

13. 經營者在設計新名稱、標識或產品等時，可以在線檢索香港和內地的官方數據庫，以了解其他經營者是否已經使用相同或相似的名稱或創意，或是否已經獲得相應的註冊。

## ▌ *專利*[18]

14. 以下發明可以享有專利保護：

    (1) 是新穎的——指在提交申請之前不為人所知；

    (2) 包含創造性——指具有非顯而易見性； 及

    (3) 能作工業應用——指能夠在任何種類的工業中製造或使用。

15. 專利需註冊，保護期限取決於所獲專利的類型和註冊地（一般最長為20年，但香港的短期專利為8年，內地的實用新型專利為10年）。

16. 如果一項發明是部分或全部在內地完成或開發，經營者應首先考慮其希望為該發明獲得哪個司法管轄區的專利保護 ( 見上文第 3 段 )：

    (1) 如果希望在內地獲得專利保護，則經營者僅需在內地提出專利申請。

    (2) 如果希望在內地以外的地方獲得專利保護，則經營者應在向相關外國司法管轄區就發明提出專利申請之前，首先取得中國國家知識產權局對申請外國專利的許可。 否則，當經營者以後在內地就該發明提出專利申請時，內地的申請可能不會被批准 [19]。

17. 如果一項發明是部分或全部在香港完成或開發，經營者僅需在香港以外的相關外國司法管轄區就該發明提出專利申請，因為香港沒有申請外國專利許可的概念。

## ▌ 註冊外觀設計 [20]

18. 註冊外觀設計是保護製成品的外觀，例如織物圖案、珠寶設計或產品包裝設計。

19. 外觀設計需註冊，註冊的有效期在香港最長為 25 年，在內地最長為 15 年。

# 侵權

20. 任何人在商品或服務中或為其業務 ( 例如在宣傳材料中 ) 複製或使用他人的知識產權，即為侵權。

21. 對侵權索賠有多種抗辯理由，例如附帶包含版權作品，或使用註冊商標以代表所註冊商標的商品或服務。

22. 根據所侵犯知識產權類別和知識產權所有權人所指稱侵權行為的不同，侵權可能引起民事責任，甚至刑事責任。

23. 另有一種稱為「假冒」的普通法訴求，旨在保護經營者的商譽和聲譽。 經營者非法不實陳述其商品或服務是其他經營者的商品或服務時，即可提起假冒的訴求。 內地也有類似的訴由，稱為「不正當競爭」。[21]

24. 在民事索賠中，香港和內地對侵權和假冒行為的救濟大體相同，均可能包括停止侵權行為的禁令、侵權聲明、損害賠償或交出所得利潤、追償合理的訴訟費用及／或交出或銷毀侵權材料。

---

[16] 《版權條例》（第528章）；《中華人民共和國著作權法》
[17] 《商標條例》（第559章）；《中華人民共和國商標法》
[18] 《專利條例》（第514章）；《中華人民共和國專利法》
[19] 《中華人民共和國專利法》第19條
[20] 《註冊外觀設計條例》（第522章）；《中華人民共和國專利法》
[21] 《中華人民共和國反不正當競爭法》

第四章　籌集資金的類型

## 概述

1. 籌集資金是任何新企業最重要的初始步驟之一。隨著企業的發展，企業的融資需求也會隨之發展。本章概述了可供香港初創企業選擇的融資方式以及初創企業申請貸款時需要考慮的關鍵問題。

2. 一般而言，企業可選擇的籌集資金方式可以分為兩大類：債務融資及股權融資。 債務融資涉及借入資金並負有義務償還債務，而股權融資則涉及通過向投資人出讓公司部分所有權換取資金。這兩種融資方式各有利弊。 債務融資的主要優勢是所有權人放棄較少的企業控制權，而股權融資的主要優勢在於沒有償還資金或就資金籌措支付任何利息或費用的義務。

3. 除私人資金外，初創企業還可受益於香港政府和其他公共機構提供的用於促進創業及支持小企業的資助計劃。

# 初創企業融資方式的主要類型

## ▌ 香港政府和其他機構提供的資助計劃

4.  在香港政府的青年發展基金下推出的「粵港澳大灣區青年創業資助計劃」資助香港的非政府機構,為在香港及大灣區創業的青年提供創業支持。該計劃通過向獲資助機構提供配對資助,為青年初創企業提供最高60萬港元的種子資金。

5.  其他政府部門、本地大學及非營利組織提供的特定計劃也提供初創資金。其中一些計劃主要惠及科技領域的初創企業。該等計劃包括:

    (1) 數碼港提供的「數碼港創意微型基金」;

    (2) 香港政府提供的「創科創投基金」;

    (3) 香港科技園提供的「Ideation 計劃」;

    (4) 香港政府提供的「大學科技初創企業資助計劃」;

    (5) 香港青年協會提供的「香港青年創業計劃」。

6.  除資金資助外,該等計劃通常包括師友導師、專業諮詢、共享辦公空間及其他對初創企業的協助。

7.  該等計劃的評審準則、要求、申請程序及審查過程各不相同。初創企業應參考相關計劃的網站以獲取進一步信息。

## ▌ 投資

8.  種子輪:初創企業最早期的資金通常來源於所有權人或其親屬和朋友的個人積蓄。

9. 天使輪：在下一個階段，初創企業可能已經開發出一個原型和一個業務模式。初創企業隨後可能會以股權或可轉換債務作為回報，尋求天使投資人的投資。天使投資人通常是富有的企業家。除提供營運資本外，天使投資人還可通過其商業網絡、人脈關係及經驗幫助初創企業。請參閱第六章第11段至第15段，了解與天使投資人有關的法律及規管問題的更多信息。

10. A 輪融資：隨著初創企業的不斷發展，可能會吸引風險資本機構的投資。 風險資本家通常獲得初創企業的股份作為投資回報。其投資的目標是通過「退出」事件而產生利潤，例如公司首次公開招股 (IPO) 或在併購 (M&A) 交易中出售股份。 A 輪融資後可能會有後續輪次的融資 ( 即 B 輪融資、C 輪融資等 )。

### ▍眾籌

11. 眾籌指向大眾籌措小額資金的在線籌集資金，可以通過商業化運營的在線平台進行。 有關眾籌的法律及規管問題的更多信息，請參閱第六章第11段至第19段。

### ▍貸款

12. 初創企業也可以考慮從金融機構 ( 例如持牌銀行 ) 及其他渠道獲取貸款。 由於銀行在批准貸款申請時通常會評估企業過去的業績，因此銀行貸款更適合於有既定業績記錄的初創企業。

## 貸款融資概述

### ▍從金融機構獲得貸款

13. 如果初創企業希望從金融機構獲得貸款為其業務相關開支提供資金，可以考慮申請商業貸款。 金融機構在決定是否批准貸款前會評估初創企業的信用。

14. 另外，個人 ( 例如初創企業的所有權人 ) 也可能從金融機構獲得個人貸款,然後將所得資金投資於初創企業。 申請個人貸款的程序及要求通常更為簡單。 但是,貸款人在批准貸款申請之前可能會評估個人的收入及信用評分。 初創企業或所有權人在考慮是否申請貸款用於為企業開支提供資金時,還應考慮如何將個人資金與企業資金分開。

15. 初創企業還可考慮其是否有資格參與香港按證保險有限公司(香港按揭證券有限公司的一家全資子公司)提供的「中小企融資擔保計劃」。該計劃通過為貸款融資提供信貸擔保,幫助本地中小企業從參與該計劃的金融機構獲得貸款,以滿足中小企業的業務需求。

16. 除「中小企融資擔保計劃」外,一些金融機構還提供指定貸款產品,為數碼、創新及科技領域的借款人提供優惠條件,以支持其發展。

## ▍*申請貸款及相關文件*

17. 申請貸款的要求不盡相同。 除申請表格外,貸款人為批准申請的目的,通常會要求初創企業提交以下文件及信息:

(1) 業務計劃;

(2) 財務及銀行報表;

(3) 企業所有權人的財務信息及身份文件;

(4) 信用記錄;

(5) 企業獲得任何其他投資或資金的詳情; 及

(6)(如果由公司申請貸款)公司的章程文件(例如公司註冊證明書、組織章程細則、董事登記冊、成員登記冊、商業登記證)及組織結構圖。

18. 在貸款獲得批准後:

(1) 貸款人將與借款人簽署一份貸款協議,列明提供貸款的條款及條件; 及

(2) 貸款人也可能要求初創企業簽署某些正式批准借款人達成貸款交易的公司授權文件(例如董事會決議)。

## ▌ 貸款條款

19. 初創企業應仔細審查貸款人準備的貸款文件並考慮其條款是否適當。 每位貸款人提供貸款融資的實際條款可能有所不同。 通常情況下,貸款協議將包含以下關鍵條款:

(1) 還款:貸款是否在貸款人提出還款要求後即時償還(即非承諾性貸款),按照規定的特定期間以分期付款的方式定期償還,還是在貸款期結束時一次性償還。

(2) 利息及費用:作為提供貸款的回報,金融機構將對借款金額收取利息,利息可以是固定利率或浮動利率(例如基於相關銀行的最優惠貸款利率)。 在香港,任何人以超過年利率48% 的實際利率借出款項均屬違法,而超過年利率36% 的實際利率,除非有其他證據證明,則可以推定為屬敲詐性。[22]任何逾期付款均可能產生違約利息。 此外,貸款人可能就提供貸款收取前期費用或管理費用,該等費用可以按照貸款金額的百分比或固定費用計算。

(3) 陳述及承諾:陳述是一種聲明,在作出之日是真實的,而承諾則是對作出或不作出某種行為的許諾。 貸款協議中的陳述可能涉及借款人的行事能力、所有權及財務狀況、借款人遵守適用的法律、所提供財務信息的準確性及完整性等。 貸款協議中的承諾也可能涉及該等事項,還可能涉及對借款人的資產設立保證或對該等資產的處置設立限制、財務信息的提供等。

20. 在承諾性貸款項下，貸款人僅可在發生違約事件（例如，陳述是不真實的或違反承諾）或任何其他特定事件後，方可要求在貸款到期之日前償還貸款。 在非承諾性貸款項下，貸款人擁有隨時要求立即償還貸款的凌駕性權利，即使借款人在融資交易中並未違約。 由於貸款人無法預料的還款要求可以嚴重影響初創企業的業務，非承諾性貸款自然對初創企業構成更大的風險。 作為回報，貸款人通常以較低的利率提供非承諾性貸款。

## 擔保及保證

21. 按照貸款人對企業和其所有權人的信用評估，以及是否有可用於支持借款人還款義務的資產，貸款人可以要求所有權人為借款人償還貸款作出擔保或提供企業或其所有權人的資產作為保證。

22. 如果借款人未能按時償還貸款，貸款人可以：

(1) 要求擔保人在貸款人提出還款要求後清償借款人所欠付的逾期款項； 及

(2) 強制執行所提供的任何保證及出售或以其他方式處理保證資產以償還貸款。

因此，初創企業應仔細考慮為企業獲得貸款作出擔保及為支持貸款提供保證的風險，並就其影響徵詢法律意見。

23. 如果：

(1) 保證是由在香港成立的公司或註冊的非香港公司提供； 及

(2) 提供保證的資產是屬於《公司條例》（第622章）中確定為可以登記的類別之一（且對於註冊的非香港公司而言，提供保證的資產位於香港），則保證文件須在香港公司註冊處登記。

24. 經核證的設立或證明資產保證的文書副本，連同按照指定表格填寫的有關該保證的詳情，須在公司設立保證之日後的一個月內提交香港公司註冊處。 如果公司未按要求提交有關指定押記的詳情，該公司和該公司的每一負責人均將被刑事起訴並處以罰款。[23]

25. 除香港公司註冊處的登記要求外，如果在位於香港或在香港登記的某些類型的資產上設立保證，從貸款人的角度而言，額外的完善、保護及／或優先權措施也是必要或適當的。 例如：

    (1) 如果是在香港的房地產上設立保證，貸款人通常會要求在香港土地註冊處進行登記； 及

    (2) 如果是在香港註冊的商標、專利或註冊設計上設立保證，貸款人可以要求在香港知識產權署的適用紀錄冊上進行登記。

26. 在內地，適用的登記要求取決於設立保證的資產類型。 例如：

    (1) 如果以在內地成立的有限責任公司的股權或在內地成立的非上市股份有限公司的股份設立質押，該質押應在標的公司成立或登記所在的市場監管局的地方機構辦理登記； 及

    (2) 如果在位於內地的房地產上設立抵押，則該抵押應在當地房地產登記處辦理登記。

27. 初創企業在同意以在內地的資產提供保證之前，應查看當地處理相關登記部門的規定和操作，以確保符合適用法律及當地通行做法。

---

[22] 自2022年12月30日起生效的經修訂的《放債人條例》（第163章）。
[23] 《公司條例》（第622章）第334條、第335條、第336條及第337條。

第五章

# 通過天使投資人及眾籌

## 開展社會化風險融資

## 概述

1. 由於缺乏既定的業績記錄，初創企業在通過傳統渠道（例如通過銀行貸款或首次公開發行）籌集資金時往往面臨重重挑戰。 天使投資人和眾籌是可供初創企業選擇的兩種替代方式。 本章討論初創企業在決定該等替代方式是否適合時應注意的主要法律及規管事項。

## 為業務籌集資金的途徑

### ▋ 甚麼是天使投資人？

2. 「天使投資人」一詞通常指富有的個人，其向認為有成功潛力的初創企業提供一次性資本投資，以換取股權（即由初創企業發行的股份）或可轉換債務（即賦予投資人要求初創企業以股份償還債務的權利）。 天使投資人的最終目標是在初創企業的業務步入正軌並實現盈利後，通過處置其持有的初創企業股份來實現其投資回報。

3. 天使投資人通常本人是企業家。 除了提供資金來源幫助處於早期階段的初創企業外，天使投資人往往樂意與初創企業分享經驗並提供有價值的指導。

4.  天使投資人可能與初創企業的創始人之間有關聯 —— 例如家人及朋友。天使投資人的其他來源包括轉介（無論是正式的還是非正式的）、為初創企業和投資人舉辦的會議及活動，或商業計劃書及項目推介材料的提交。

## ■ 甚麼是眾籌？

5.  就初創企業而言，「眾籌」一詞指使用從大眾（無論是個人還是組織）獲取的小額款項為初創企業的業務提供資金。

6.  初創企業可以通過第三方運營的在線眾籌平台獲得眾籌，或自行獲取眾籌。

7.  常見的商業眾籌類型包括：

    (1) 股權眾籌，指投資人向初創企業投資，以換取該初創企業發行的股份或債務票據的權益，或分享集體投資計劃架構的眾籌安排所產生的利潤或收入的權益。

    (2) 點對點 (P2P) 借貸，指眾籌平台將貸款人（投資人）與初創企業配對，以向初創企業提供無擔保貸款。

    (3) 報酬 / 預售性質的眾籌，指貸款人可以在適當時從初創企業獲得實物商品或服務，而非權益或貨幣形式的回報。

8.  初創企業通常認為眾籌具有吸引力，因為其提供相對容易且成本較低的機會接觸到大量投資人，提升初創企業在市場上的知名度，及允許初創企業保留控制權。

# 相關法律及法規

## ▌ *尚無單個特定法例或規管體系*

9. 香港的法律及法規允許天使投資及眾籌並對其進行規管。相關的規管要求由多個法規規定。目前尚無適用於天使投資或眾籌的單個特定法例或規管體系。

10. 因此，初創企業應在考量自身相關事實及情況的基礎上，注意適用的法律及法規。

## ▌ *與提供投資 / 從投資人獲得資金有關的法律及法規*

11. 《公司 ( 清盤及雜項條文 ) 條例》[24] 載有如下文意的規定：

(1) 初創企業用於向公眾發售股份或債券證 ( 包括債權股證、債券及任何其他債務證券 ) 的文件相當於招股章程，須包含規定的內容並遵守《公司 ( 清盤及雜項條文 ) 條例》的登記要求。

(2)「招股章程」一詞在《公司 ( 清盤及雜項條文 ) 條例》中含有廣泛的定義，包括招股章程、通知、通告、冊子、廣告或其他文件。

(3)《公司 ( 清盤及雜項條文 ) 條例》對招股章程的要求相當苛刻。在這種情況下，初創企業往往會探索是否有可供適用的豁免或安全港，避免受制於該等要求，並根據自身特有的事實及情況，評估其在實踐中是否可以依賴該等豁免或安全港。

(4) 豁免或安全港載於《公司 ( 清盤及雜項條文 ) 條例》的附表 17。 在遵守《公司 ( 清盤及雜項條文 ) 條例》施加的其他要求及條件的前提下，可能與初創企業有關的豁免或安全港包括：

(a) 向「專業投資者」（其定義見《證券及期貨條例》[25]）發出的要約；

(b) 向50人或更少的人數發出的要約（即私募安全港）；

(c) 須為有關股份或債權證支付的總代價不超過5,000,000港元的要約（即低面額安全港）；及

(d) 某人士應付的最低面額或本金款額或代價不低於500,000港元的要約（即高面額安全港）。

12. 《證券及期貨條例》第103條載有如下文意的規定：

(1) 任何人士發送任何廣告、邀請或文件，而該廣告、邀請或文件屬或載有邀請公眾取得證券（包括在香港境外註冊成立的初創企業所發行的股份或債務票據）或參加集體投資計劃的內容，即屬犯罪，除非該發送已獲香港證監會認可或適用豁免。

(2) 但是，《證券及期貨條例》對第103(1)條的要求作出了明確的豁免。 雖然該等豁免在一定程度上類似於《公司（清盤及雜項條文）條例》所規定的豁免或安全港，但《證券及期貨條例》及《公司（清盤及雜項條文）條例》豁免之間的關聯與相互關係並不簡單明瞭。 例如，《證券及期貨條例》規定了專業投資者豁免，但涉及私募、低面額投資或高面額投資的安排卻未明確豁免於第103(1)條的要求。

13. 根據《證券及期貨條例》，某些類型的活動可以視為受規管活動：

(1) 某些類型的活動在《證券及期貨條例》下定義為受規管活動。 在未經香港證監會發牌進行相關類型受規管活動的情況下經營或顯示自己經營受規管活動，即屬犯罪。[26]

(2) 如果初創企業正考慮使用第三方提供的眾籌平台或專業服務，應確保相關第三方平台或服務提供商持有運營或提供該等平台或服務必要的牌照。可能適用於該等第三方的牌照規定包括：

(a) 第1類（證券交易）

(b) 第4類（就證券提供意見）

(c) 第6類（就機構融資提供意見）

(d) 第9類（提供資產管理）

(3) 最有可能與初創企業直接相關的受規管活動的類型是第1類（證券交易）。

(4) 值得注意的是，香港證監會目前只向一個眾籌平台發牌經營第1類及第4類受規管活動。

## ▌ *打擊洗錢／恐怖分子資金籌集的影響及考量*

14. 根據《有組織及嚴重罪行條例》[27]、《販毒（追討得益）條例》[28] 及《聯合國（反恐怖主義措施）條例》[29]，某些融資活動可能構成犯罪活動：

    (1)《有組織及嚴重罪行條例》：處理知道或有合理理由相信為可公訴罪行的得益的任何財產，即屬犯罪。[30]

    (2)《販毒（追討得益）條例》：處理知道或有合理理由相信為販毒得益的任何財產，即屬犯罪。[31]

    (3)《聯合國（反恐怖主義措施）條例》：任何人士不得直接或間接地處理知道或罔顧屬恐怖分子財產的財產。[32]

(4) 初創企業應妥善核實資金來源，以確保其不違反上述法規。

15. 另外，值得注意的是《打擊洗錢及恐怖分子資金籌集條例》及以下事項 [33]：

(1) 雖然《打擊洗錢及恐怖分子資金籌集條例》並不直接適用於初創企業，但香港的銀行在處理賬戶開立時須遵守《打擊洗錢及恐怖分子資金籌集條例》的規定。因此，在銀行處理初創企業開立銀行賬戶的申請時，初創企業應有預期銀行會將《打擊洗錢及恐怖分子資金籌集條例》的要求轉嫁給初創企業。

(2)《打擊洗錢及恐怖分子資金籌集條例》對銀行施加多項有關客戶盡職審查 (CDD) 及備存記錄的要求，適用於與客戶建立業務關係之前及其後處理客戶的交易及帳戶。[34]

(3) 在計劃開立銀行帳戶用以持有來自天使投資人或眾籌的資金時，初創企業應對其投資人開展相應的盡職審查並核實資金來源。[35]

## ▋ *最新發展：關於眾籌活動規管的公眾諮詢*

16. 2022年12月19日，香港財經事務及庫務局（「香港財庫局」）公佈了一份諮詢文件（「諮詢文件」）[36]，就有關加強眾籌活動規管的建議開展了為期3個月的公眾諮詢。

17. 正如香港財庫局所解釋，目的是建立一個全面的機制，以增強公眾對參與合法正當的眾籌活動（無論是線上還是線下）的信心，防止不法分子以眾籌的名義從事欺詐、損害公共利益或危害公共和國家安全的活動。

18. 雖然現階段還沒有跡象顯示立法及實施的時間表，但初創企業應繼續關注相關發展。

19. 擬議的眾籌規管制度具有以下主要特點：

(1) 設立一個眾籌事務辦公室，集中處理和協調與眾籌活動有關的規管及行政事務，並負責監察眾籌活動的開展，以達到 (a) 任何人士在開展向香港個人或實體，或向位於香港的個人或實體籌集資金的眾籌活動之前，需向眾籌事務辦公室提出申請，無論該人士在香港或在香港境外開展眾籌活動； (b) 申請人需提供有關其自身的信息及擬議眾籌活動的詳情 ( 例如目標及安排 ) 以及眾籌事務辦公室要求的其他信息。

(2) 考慮對社會廣泛認可的眾籌活動或慈善性眾籌項目適用豁免及簡化措施，以促進其及時啟動及順利運作。

(3) 鑑於線上眾籌平台的運作方式千差萬別，且通常在香港以外地區設立，考慮是否建立眾籌平台的登記制度及評估其覆蓋面和運作的操作性。

(4) 授予執法部門制止非法眾籌活動及檢控違法人士的權力。

(5) 就市場上已受金融規管機構規管且受現有法律和法規規管的商業籌集資金活動，豁免適用擬議的眾籌規管制度。

## 所需的文件

20. 根據投資架構及其他因素的差異，在籌集資金方面可能使用的文件在不同情況下各不相同。以下討論一些主要文件供一般性參考。法律文件及合同的談判對初創企業非常重要，須確保合同條款反映初創企業的意願及需求，且保護初創企業及其創始人、現有股東及管理團隊的權益。初創企業應考慮在必要時尋求專業顧問的幫助。

21. 與天使投資有關的一些主要文件包括：

(1) 募資資料包 —— 即一份演示資料包，其中包含可行且可持續性的業務計劃、業務及增長戰略、關鍵團隊成員和僱員、擬籌集的資金款額、財務狀況、公司基本信息等，以引起潛在投資者的興趣。

(2) 條款清單 —— 該清單通常是在談判啟動前由初創企業或天使投資人準備，用以列出關鍵的投資條款，例如投資金額、如何使用投資金額、天使投資人將獲得的回報、是否保留或共享管理控制權（及如何保留或共享），關鍵或有價值資產（例如知識產權）的所有權等。

(3) 認購協議 / 股東協議 —— 這是由初創企業（及其現有股東（如適用））與天使投資人簽署的一份主要法律合同，規定二者之間的關係（包括該等關係的建立、維持及終止）。該合同正式列明投資條款及各方的權利和義務。

(4) 初創企業的組織章程細則 —— 根據不同的投資安排，初創企業可能需要修改其組織章程細則或同等的章程文件，以進行股份分配、不同類別股份（如適用）的分配或（經天使投資人要求）明確規定天使投資人對各項事務享有的權利（例如對其投資獲得股息或回報的權利、參與或控制公司管理的權利、退出權等）。

22. 與眾籌有關的一些主要文件包括：

(1) 募資資料包——即一份演示資料包，其中包含可行且可持續性的業務計劃、業務及增長戰略、關鍵團隊成員和僱員、擬籌集的資金款額、財務狀況、公司基本信息等，以引起潛在投資者的興趣。

(2) 籌集資金協議 / 認購協議 / 股東協議 — 這是由初創企業（及

其現有股東（如適用））與貸款人（或匯集貸款人的投資工具）簽署的一份主要法律合同，規定初創企業及貸款人之間的關係（包括該等關係的建立、維持及終止）。該合同正式列明投資條款及各方的權利和義務。

---

24　《公司（清盤及雜項條文）條例》，香港法例第 32 章
25　《證券及期貨條例》，香港法例第 571 章
26　《證券及期貨條例》第 114 條
27　《有組織及嚴重罪行條例》，香港法例第 455 章
28　《販毒（追討得益）條例》，香港法例第 405 章
29　《聯合國（反恐怖主義措施）條例》，香港法例第 575 章
30　《有組織及嚴重罪行條例》第 25 條
31　《販毒（追討得益）條例》第 25 條
32　《聯合國（反恐怖主義措施）條例》第 8A 條
33　《打擊洗錢及恐怖分子資金籌集條例》，香港法例第 615 章
34　《打擊洗錢及恐怖分子資金籌集條例》附表 2
35　《2022 年打擊洗錢及恐怖分子資金籌集（修訂）條例》並未改變《打擊洗錢及恐怖分子資金籌集條例》中關於銀行客戶盡職審查及備存記錄的要求。因此，《打擊洗錢及恐怖分子資金籌集條例》規定的初創企業應採取合理措施以開展相應的盡職審查及核實其投資人資金來源的義務仍繼續適用。
36　諮詢文件可以在以下網址查看：https://www.fstb.gov.hk/fsb/sc/publication/consult/doc/Crowdfunding_consultation_paper_Chi_final.pdf

## 第六章 爭議解決

### 概述

1. 香港的民事司法系統為當事人解決爭議提供了一系列的既定程序。 傳統的法院訴訟只是其中的一種途徑。 爭議解決的替代模式是調解和仲裁。 該三種選擇各有其明顯的優缺點。 本章闡述傳統的爭議解決模式和替代的爭議解決模式。

### 調解

2. 在香港，調解是一個非正式、雙方合意、保密的程序，特點是有一名公正的調解員。 調解員並不控制爭議解決過程的結果。 相反，調解員的作用是促進當事人解決爭議本身，或至少嘗試縮小當事人的分歧。 律師參與調解不是必需的。 即使律師到場代表當事人行事，其在調解過程中所起的作用也相對較小。 在調解過程中達成和解後，當事人可以根據訴訟是否已經啟動，簽署一份具有約束力的和解協議，或將和解條款納入一份經雙方同意的判決或命令。 如果一方違反和解協議的條款，另一方可以向香港法院出示和解協議，並請求法院根據所達成的和解協議條款作出命令。

3.  完全或部分沒有律師的參與意味著與法院訴訟和仲裁相比，調解的費用相對較低。 由於調解期間的談話內容是保密的，當事人通常更願意暢所欲言，並可能願意透露其底線。 非正式的氛圍也意味著對各方的壓力較小，通常有利於更和諧地交換意見。但是，如果一方沒有解決爭議的真實意向，只是想避免法院訴訟或仲裁，調解程序就可能作為一種拖延策略被濫用。

4.  在現代民事糾紛中，調解通常是當事人解決任何形式爭議的第一步。 即使當事人不以調解作為第一步，香港法院也有指引鼓勵當事人至少嘗試進行調解。[37]

5.  經當事人同意，內地法院也可能進行調解[38]。在當事人達成和解後，內地法院可以製作正式調解書以記錄和解條款，該調解書與法院判決一樣可以強制執行[39]。 任何當事人均不能對調解書提出上訴，但如果一方有證據證明通過調解達成的和解違反自願原則，或當事人達成的和解條款違反法律，則該方可以申請再審以撤銷正式調解書。[40]

## 訴訟

6.  除非當事人達成仲裁協議，當事人如果調解不成，將不得不通過法院訴訟解決爭議。在訴訟方面，香港法院系統指定的審裁處和法院根據索賠金額和所尋求的救濟享有相應的管轄權，可以解決幾乎所有類型的糾紛。

7.  就純金錢索賠而言，解決爭議的適當平台取決於索賠的金額：

    (1) 小額錢債審裁處[41]處理金額不超過75,000港元的金錢索賠。律師不得參與，庭審通常以粵語進行。

    (2) 區域法院[42]處理超過75,000港元但不超過300萬港元的純金錢索賠，以及對中小金額合同尋求衡平法救濟的非金錢索賠等，例如強制履行[43]。雖然當事人可以作為無律師代表的訴訟人親自出庭（即在沒有律師代表的情況下出庭），但由於程序和案件本身可能相當複雜，當事人大多委託律師代表其出庭。

(3) 高等法院原訟法庭[44]具有無限的司法管轄權，可以審理和裁定金額超過300萬港元的索賠。

8.　一般而言，不同法院的民事訴訟程序是相似的，可以歸納如下：

(1) 狀書——當事人需以書面形式陳述各自案件的事實背景。

(2) 文件披露——作為審前程序，各方需向另一方披露其持有、保管或控制的與爭議有關的文件。

(3) 證人陳述書——當事人可能希望法院在對爭議作出判決前考慮證人的口頭證供。這可以通過準備證人陳述書實現，證人陳述書的內容可以作為當事人在審訊中的主問證據，證人可以在庭審中接受盤問。

(4) 審訊——取決於案件的複雜程度，法院通常在審訊時處理爭議，由律師為當事人陳述案情，證人需提供口頭證供並接受盤問。法院在公開審訊的通常情況下，一般允許公眾（包括媒體）出席旁聽整個審訊過程。

(5) 判決——在聽取當事人律師的陳述和證人的證詞後，法院通過判決說明相關理由並對爭議做出有利於勝訴方的裁決。一般而言，勝訴方可以向敗訴方索賠部分的律師費用。

(6) 上訴——敗訴方可以在法院規則規定的時間內向上級法院提起上訴。通常有兩次上訴權。

9.　在取得判決後，勝訴方可以著手進行強制執行程序（見下文第19段）。

10. 在內地，從管轄範圍最小的最低層級到管轄範圍不設限的最高層級，大致有四級法院：基層人民法院、市中級人民法院、省高級人民法院和最高人民法院。

11. 對這些法院的地域和級別管轄權有一系列具體的規則。簡而言之，大多數初創企業的爭議案件很可能是由基層人民法院處理。基層人民法院有權審理和裁定標的為人民幣1億元或以下以及在某些情況下達到人民幣5億元的案件（國內案件），並有權審理和裁定標的為人民幣2,000萬元至4,000萬元的案件（涉外案件）。敗訴方可以在法律規定的時間內向上級法院提起上訴。通常只有一次上訴權，但在特殊情況下，受害方可以申請對上訴法院的判決進行再審或重審。

12. 在內地，訴訟案件通常由三名審判員組成合議庭進行審理[45]。但是，在基層人民法院，對於「事實清楚，權利義務關係明確，爭議不大」的案件，或當事人約定適用簡易程序的案件，可以由審判員一人獨任審理。[46]在簡易程序中作出的涉及小額訴訟（標的額因城市而異，從人民幣3萬元到7萬元不等）的判決是一審終審，不能上訴[47]。

13. 中文是內地法院訴訟的唯一官方語言[48]。所有向法院提交的外文文件都須翻譯成中文[49]。

14. 與香港不同，內地沒有「普通法式」的證據披露或證人陳述書交換的程序。當事人無需提交不利於自身利益的證據。內地法院並不強調當事人的口頭證供，也因而通常不要求交換證人陳述書。

## 仲裁

15. 如果談判或調解不成功，但雙方之間已達成仲裁協議，則爭議須提交仲裁解決。

16. 仲裁是一個雙方合意、保密的程序,由仲裁庭裁定爭議的結果。一般而言,當事人可以同意指定一名或三名仲裁員組成「仲裁庭」。仲裁地和仲裁程序所適用的規則應包含在仲裁協議中。與調解不同,仲裁程序通常具有上文第8(1)段至第8(5)段所述法院程序的特點。

17. 在仲裁程序的實體問題開庭審理中,仲裁庭在聽取了當事人代理律師的陳述和證人的證詞後,以「仲裁裁決」的方式對爭議作出有利於勝訴方的裁決。除少數例外情形[50],仲裁裁決是最終的,不能上訴或覆核。因此,仲裁通常比法院訴訟更快捷、更便宜。

18. 在內地,仲裁也是一種普遍的、替代訴訟的解決爭議方式。內地的仲裁程序在某些方面與香港的仲裁程序不同,而且一般而言比香港的仲裁程序更快捷、更便宜。

## 強制執行

19. 在取得判決或仲裁裁決(視情況而定)後,勝訴方可以對敗訴方執行香港法院的判決或仲裁裁決(如同法院判決一樣)。關鍵的是,敗訴方在香港是否有任何可供執行的資產。如果有可供執行的資產,一些常見的執行方式包括:

(1) 扣押敗訴方銀行帳戶的資金或第三方欠付敗訴方的資金,以全部或部分償付所欠的判定債務。[51]

(2) 扣押不動產或公司股份等財產,直至全部清償判定債務為止[52];

(3) 法院執達主任扣押敗訴方的動產[53];

(4) 敗訴方的清盤(如為公司)或破產(如為個人)[54]。

20. 內地的個人破產與香港相似,雖然個人破產已經在包括深圳在內的多個城市進行了試點,但在內地仍是一個相對較新的概念。

21. 除少數例外情形外,香港法院通常會承認並執行符合協議管轄要求(即在相關合同中以書面形式明確約定內地法院具有唯一管轄權)的內地法院所作的金錢判決或在內地根據《仲裁法》作出的仲裁裁決。同樣,內地法院也承認並普遍執行符合協議管轄要求(即在相關合同中以書面形式明確約定香港法院具有唯一管轄權)的香港法院作出的金錢判決或在香港作出的仲裁裁決。跨境執行安排的具體信息載於以下文件:

    (1)《關於內地與香港特別行政區法院相互認可和執行當事人協議管轄的民商事案件判決的安排》[55];

    (2)《關於內地與香港特別行政區相互執行仲裁裁決的安排》。

---

[37] 《高等法院規則》(第4A章),第1A號命令第4(e)條規則;實務指示31——「調解」。

[38] 《中華人民共和國民事訴訟法》(2021年修訂)第96條。

[39] 《中華人民共和國民事訴訟法》(2021年修訂)第100條。

[40] 《中華人民共和國民事訴訟法》(2021年修訂)第208條。

[41] 《小額錢債審裁處條例》(第338章)。

[42] 《區域法院條例》(第336章)。

[43] 財產購買協議的強制履行程序,購買價款不超過300萬港元,如果該協議與土地有關,購買價款不超過700萬港元。

[44] 《高等法院條例》(第4章)

[45] 《中華人民共和國民事訴訟法》(2021年修訂)第40條和第41條。

[46] 《中華人民共和國民事訴訟法》(2021年修訂)第160條。

[47] 《中華人民共和國民事訴訟法》(2021年修訂)第165條。

[48] 《中華人民共和國民事訴訟法》(2021年修訂)第269條。

[49] 《中華人民共和國民事訴訟法》(2021年修訂)第73條。

[50] 例如,當事人已事先通過簽訂協議明確約定,可以以「嚴重不當事件」或「法律問題」為由就仲裁裁決向法院提出異議。

[51] 《高等法院規則》(第4A章),第49號命令。

[52] 《高等法院規則》(第4A章),第50號命令。

[53] 《高等法院規則》(第4A章),第47號命令。

[54] 《公司(清盤及雜項條文)條例》(第32章);《破產條例》(第6章)。

[55] 根據律政司網站 (https://www.doj.gov.hk/sc/mainland_and_macao/RRECCJ.html),該安排將被最高人民法院與香港特別行政區政府於2019年1月18日簽署的《關於內地與香港特別行政區法院相互認可和執行民商事案件判決的安排》所取代,屆時香港將製定本地立法。新安排將擴大相互認可和執行判決的範圍,例如,包括某些類型的非金錢判決,並以其他不太苛刻的條件取代唯一管轄權的條件。

# 香港青年協會

hkfyg.org.hk | m21.hk

香港青年協會(簡稱青協)於1960年成立,是香港最具規模的青年服務機構。隨著社會瞬息萬變,青年所面對的機遇和挑戰時有不同,而青協一直不離不棄,關愛青年並陪伴他們一同成長。本著以青年為本的精神,我們透過專業服務和多元化活動,培育年青一代發揮潛能,為社會貢獻所長。至今每年使用我們服務的人次達600萬。在社會各界支持下,我們全港設有80多個服務單位,全面支援青年人的需要,並提供學習、交流和發揮創意的平台。此外,青協登記會員人數已逾45萬;而為推動青年發揮互助精神、實踐公民責任的青年義工網絡,亦有逾23萬登記義工。在「青協 · 有您需要」的信念下,我們致力拓展12項核心服務,全面回應青年的需要,並為他們提供適切服務,包括:青年空間、M21媒體服務、就業支援、邊青服務、輔導服務、家長服務、領袖培訓、義工服務、教育服務、創意交流、文康體藝及研究出版。

e·Giving

青協網上捐款平台

# 香港青年協會
# 社會創新及青年創業部簡介

香港青年協會社會創新及青年創業部不但為青年提
供創業和社會創新的教育及培訓，並為有意創業之
青年提供實際財務及多元化的服務，以實踐創業理
想，同時鼓勵青年運用創新點子來解決社會問題，
並建立商業營運的可持續模式，從而改善社會現狀。

## ■ 孵化培育

透過推出不同的培育計劃及培訓，為初創者提供創
業啟動金、辦公空間、創業導師及培訓等資源，減
低其經濟負擔。

## ▌香港青年創業計劃

「香港青年創業計劃」由2005年開始獲得黃廷方慈善基金支持,為香港的創業青年提供一站式服務。計劃更為青年創業家提供最高港幣十五萬元免息貸款。自創立以來,計劃收到共2,293份申請,共有240份申請獲得通過批核,支持青年企業的免息貸款金額累計港幣17,424,570元。

此計劃為青年創業家提供免費商業諮詢服務,顧問團隊由資深創業家、工商界高級行政人員、顧問及專業人士組成,他們貢獻時間、專業知識和經驗,有助青年創業家改善商業的營運。計劃亦與「青年創業國際計劃」緊密聯繫。

## ▌商業指導

商業指導目的是為青年創業家提供業務支援,切合不同業務需要,協助他們尋找適合的業務改善方案。青年創業家先向專業導師介紹業務及點子,再與專業導師進一步討論業務狀況。專業導師來自不同背景和行業,針對疑難雜症作出建議及支援。

## ▌網絡支援

透過舉辦各類型青年創業學培訓課程、創業家講座、分享會及聚會,滙集不同行業人士參與,以鞏固基礎的社會創新及創業理論和知識、並提供業務轉介機會,擴闊初創業務網絡。為了協助青年創業家展示業務,青協賽馬會社會創新中心定期舉辦各類型活動,以幫助他們擴展業務網絡、增加曝光率,並接觸不同行業的專家及商界精英。

## ▌香港青年協會賽馬會社會創新中心

香港青年協會賽馬會社會創新中心於2015年成立，位於黃竹坑活化工廈創協坊（Genesis），鄰近港鐵黃竹坑站，佔地近5,000平方呎，設施及基本工程裝置承蒙香港賽馬會慈善信託基金捐助。截至2023年，已為超過80間初創公司及超過200位青年創業家提供共享空間、商務辦公室及創業培育支援。

## ▌粵港澳大灣區支援

青協是前海深港青年夢工場的發起機構之一。我們與大灣區各孵化中心建立緊密聯繫，提名香港優秀的初創企業到大灣區發展業務。

2021年，青協主辦的「粵港澳大灣區青年創業先行者」，獲得民政及青年事務局及青年發展委員會的青年發展基金轄下「粵港澳大灣區青年創業資助計劃」資助，是《青創同行 We Venture》旗下項目，為12隊初創團隊提供3年孵化服務。青協於2023年與大灣區9個內地城市共27間合作夥伴正式簽訂戰略合作協議。

# 孖士打律師行

孖士打律師行（孖士打）是一家獨特的全球律師行，專為世界領先企業和金融機構在極為複雜的交易和爭議中提供法律諮詢服務。

孖士打在全球主要商業中心設有 27 個辦事處並擁有 1,800 多名律師，網路覆蓋四大洲。 我們為客戶提供深入的當地市場知識和實在的全球服務，使我們能夠為其業務提供最佳的解決方案。我們的「一行」文化，即所有業務領域和地區之間的無縫融合，可確保客戶能夠獲得最佳的服務品質。

孖士打植根於香港，是香港規模最大、歷史最悠久的律師行之一，自1863年以來一直支援本地企業，並持續服務香港社會。位於交通便利的中環，我們擁有超過 60名合夥人100多名律師，在包括銀行及金融、化工、能源、保險、生命科學、房地產及科技等眾多業務領域上執業，為客戶提供全面和綜合的法律服務。

自90年代開始，我們通過北京和上海的代表處為客戶在中國內地提供支援。憑藉扎實的國際經驗以及對外商投資和對外投資法律框架的深入了解，我們能夠啟動我們全球律師行的力量將我們的律師團隊與遍佈全球的客戶聯繫起來為其服務。

我們在廣泛的業務領域提供優質的法律服務，包括：

- 反壟斷及競爭法

- 銀行及金融
- 資本市場
- 公司及證券
- 跨境合併及收購
- 網路安全及數據隱私
- 新興公司及風險投資
- 僱傭及福利
- 企業風險及危機管理
- 金融服務監管及執行
- 全球調查及白領犯罪辯護
- 知識產權
- 國際貿易
- 合資企業及戰略聯盟
- 訴訟及爭議解決
- 外包
- 房地產市場
- 重組
- 稅務
- 技術及知識產權交易

我們多元化的律師團隊具有敏銳的商業觸覺，並致力於提供卓越的服務，被客戶視為戰略合作夥伴。

在香港提供社區服務是孖士打傳統的重要組成部分。多年來，我們的律師和其他員工一直熱衷於尋求機會為有需要人士以及其所屬的組織提供支援。我們通過參與公益法律服務及企業社會責任活動來實現這個目標。我們堅信這是律師行業的重要組成部分，也是我們作為律師行實現真正卓越的重要一環。

我們履行公益法律服務義務其中重要的途徑是向教育相關的計劃和組織提供支援。例如，我們的律師一直與香港青年協會不同的單位保持著合作關係。除了與香港青年創業計劃共同編制本《法律指南》外，我們的律師還被委任為香港青年創業計劃的評審團成員，負責從法律角度評審香港和大灣區青年創業者的商業計劃書。

企業社會責任是我們回饋社會及幫助有需要人士的另一個途徑。我們相信每當社區繁榮興盛時，我們也可蓬勃發展。每一年，我們都探討如何在世界和我們周圍的事物產生積極影響的方向來制定我們的企業社會責任計劃。我們參與了眾多的社會活動，其中包括清理行山徑、支持用於淨化海水的牡蠣養殖、向貧困社區分發膳食以及指導有特殊教育需求的年輕人等。疫情期間，我們多位同事挺身而出，積極參加各種義工活動，包括在全港派發抗疫包、探訪獨居長者等，幫助解決社會的燃眉之急。

如需了解更多信息，請訪問我們的網站
www.mayerbrown.com。

# 鳴謝

## 孖士打律師行

**商業載體**

容璟瑜｜馬譽庭｜周一舟

**僱傭**

譚卓詠｜勞敏嘉

**知識產權**

余嘉威｜黃忻

**籌集資金的類型**

駱允莊｜賀子晴

**通過天使投資人及眾籌開展**
**社會化風險融資**

柯倩文｜霍晧生｜張叡文

**爭議解決**

董光顯｜楊春雷

羅永逸｜黃欣

## 香港青年協會

鄧良順｜李綺蓮

# 免責聲明

本《法律指南》由孖士打律師行及香港青年協會通力協作編制。本《法律指南》的內容僅為相關事項提供一般性指引，不可理解為法律、會計、財務、稅務或其他專業的建議或意見。本《法律指南》不能替代針對個別情況出具的特定建議或意見，也不應視為可取代法律或其他持牌專業人士的專業意見。本《法律指南》的作者、編輯和出版商均不對本《法律指南》的內容的準確性、及時性、完整性或適用性作出任何形式的陳述或保證，並且不會對任何個人或實體就任何因本《法律指南》提供的資訊，或因使用該等資訊而承擔任何形式的法律責任或基於任何原因所造成或引致的任何直接、間接、附帶、或相應的損失或損害。本《法律指南》的銷售代表或推廣員或任何書面銷售材料均無權創立或提供任何保證。所有損失或損害的風險均由讀者獨自承擔，而且所有責任在此被明確排除。

本《法律指南》於2023年6月16日編制，其內容將隨著法律和法規（以及對該等法律和法規的解釋）的改動而變動。法律和法規（以及對該等法律和法規的解釋）的改動可能會導致重大的法律後果，而且考慮到每家公司的不同情況，本《法律指南》提供的資訊可能亦不適用於所有公司。讀者在採取本《法律指南》所討論事項相關的任何行動之前，應尋求獨立的法律意見或其他專業意見。

除非另有說明，本《法律指南》的所有版權及其他知識產權均屬孖士打律師行及香港青年協會所有。本《法律指南》可下載或列印作私人用途，或在個別公司或組織內供私人閱覽，或僅供在該公司或組織內閱覽之用。任何個人或實體未經孖士打律師行及香港青年協會的事先書面同意，不得將本《法律指南》的資訊複製或分發給任何協力廠商，亦不得將本《法律指南》用於商業目的。

# 創業法律指南 III

| | |
|---|---|
| 出版 | 香港青年協會 |
| 訂購及查詢 | 香港北角百福道 21 號 |
| | 香港青年協會大廈 21 樓 |
| | 專業叢書統籌組 |
| 電話 | (852) 3755 7108 |
| 傳真 | (852) 3755 7155 |
| 電郵 | cps@hkfyg.org.hk |
| 網頁 | hkfyg.org.hk |
| 網上書店 | books.hkfyg.org.hk |
| M21 網台 | M21.hk |
| 版次 | 二零二三年七月初版 |
| 國際書號 | 978-988-76280-8-8 |
| 定價 | 港幣 80 元 |
| 顧問 | 何永昌先生，MH |
| 督印 | 徐小曼 |
| 作者 | 孖士打律師行 |
| 編輯委員會 | 鄧良順、黃好儀 |
| 執行編輯 | 李綺蓮、周若琦、余晴峯 |
| 實習編輯 | 許綺霖、廖小暢、蔡旻羲 |
| 設計及排版 | Axel C. |
| 製作及承印 | 宏亞印務有限公司 |

青協 APP・立即下載

CONTENT

066 — 067   Foreword

068 — 078   Chapter01——Business Vehicles

079 — 088   Chapter02——Employment

089 — 092   Chapter03——Intellectual Property ("IP") Rights, namely
            Copyright, Trade Mark, Patent, and Registered Designs

093 — 099   Chapter04——Types of Fund Raising

100 — 107   Chapter05——Social Venture Funding through Angel
            Investors and Crowdfunding

108 — 114   Chapter06——Dispute Resolution

115         About The Hong Kong Federation of Youth Groups

116 — 118   About The HKFYG Social Innovation and
            Youth Business Unit

119 — 121   About Mayer Brown

122         Contributors

123         Disclaimer

# Foreword

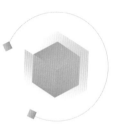

## Equip yourself with the legal knowledge to start your business endeavours

To many young entrepreneurs, corporation law and regulations seem obscure and too complicated to follow.

However, knowing your legal rights and understanding your company's legal obligations are indispensable skills for young entrepreneurs.

For example, how to decide and register your legal entity when setting up businesses in Hong Kong and the cities of the Greater Bay Area (GBA)? How to prepare employment contracts and ordinances based on different regions? How to safeguard your I intellectual property such as copyright and trademarks when new products are launched? As your startup expands, how to take legal steps to raise funds and seek venture capital funding? If there are any disputes in your company's agreement with other parties, how to take legal action to resolve the problem?

To answer these and many other questions, The Hong Kong Federation of Youth Groups is honoured to partner with Mayer Brown in producing, The Legal Guide for Business Starters III. The book serves as a legal guide to young entrepreneurs, providing legal and business knowledge and checklists to help them to start a business in Hong Kong and the GBA. With the help of the Guide, young entrepreneurs can make direct application of the knowledge to their business and avoid legal pitfalls.

I highly recommend this Legal Guide to all young entrepreneurs. With this in hand, we believe you will be on the right path to successful entrepreneurship!

Andy HO Wing-cheong, MH
Executive Director, The Hong Kong Federation of Youth Groups

# Foreword

Over the past two decades, the Hong Kong Government, the Non-Governmental Organisations and the business sector have gradually made available more financial resources and developed incubation and mentorship programmes to support our youths to launch their own businesses in Hong Kong. Among the supporters in this arena is Youth Business Hong Kong of The Hong Kong Federation of Youth Groups, which has published the Legal Guide for Business Starters in 2007 and 2014 as a tool for young entrepreneurs to navigate the legal framework when starting their businesses.

Now in its third edition, the Legal Guide is designed to provide a holistic overview of the areas that our youths would generally encounter legal issues when starting a business under the current legal framework.[1] It covers commonly encountered issues falling into categories like corporate, employment, intellectual property, finance and dispute resolution. Recognising the opportunities for a Hong Kong business to expand into the Greater Bay Area, these issues are also briefly addressed in the context of the laws in the Mainland.

An understanding of the legal considerations sets the ground for good governance, sustainability and ultimately, success of the business. The Legal Guide is meant to serve as a useful resource for the budding young entrepreneurs, the scaling start-ups and the supporters for business starters in Hong Kong.

Mayer Brown has collaborated with The Hong Kong Federation of Youth Groups to develop this edition of the Legal Guide, the contents of which are intended to provide a general guide to the subject matter only and are not intended to provide legal advice or be a substitute for specific advice concerning individual situations. Readers should seek legal advice before taking any action with respect to the matters discussed in this Legal Guide.

---

[1]As at 1 July 2023.

Terence Tung
Senior Partner, Mayer Brown

# Business Vehicles

## General

1. One of the first steps for start-ups is to establish a business vehicle for its operations. This Chapter introduces the common types of business vehicles in Hong Kong.

2. The most commonly used business vehicle in Hong Kong is a private company limited by shares. It is the focus of this Chapter.

## Common Types of Business Vehicles

3. The choice of business vehicles depends on a number of factors, such as the scale of the business, management structure, sourcing of funding, risk appetite, flexibility, etc. The most common types of business vehicles in Hong Kong are:

   (1) a private company

   (2) a partnership and

   (3) a sole proprietorship.

4. The most common types of business vehicles in the Mainland are similar to those in Hong Kong, though some of the terminologies are different.

## ▌ *Private Company*

5. A private company is a separate legal entity from its shareholders. This means that, in principle, the liability of each shareholder is limited to the amount (if any) unpaid on the shares held by that shareholder.

6. The number of shareholders in a private company is limited to 50 (not including employees and former employees). A private company is prohibited from sending any invitation to the public to subscribe for any of its shares. There are restrictions on the right of a shareholder to transfer his or her shares in the private company.

7. In the Mainland, the type of business vehicle that is closest to a private company is the limited liability company (the "LLC"). It is also a separate legal entity and the liability of each shareholder is limited to the amount of the registered capital subscribed by that shareholder. The number of shareholders in an LLC is also limited to 50. The equity interest in an LLC may be freely transferable among the shareholders, but transfers to third parties are restricted.

## ▌ *Partnership*

8. Partnerships can be formed in Hong Kong either as a general partnership or a limited partnership.

9. A Hong Kong general partnership does not have a separate legal personality. This means that partners have unlimited personal liability for the liabilities of the partnership their liabilities are not limited to their capital contribution to the partnership.

10. The main features of a Mainland general partnership are similar to those of a Hong Kong general partnership.

11. Partnerships in the Mainland can also be formed as a special general partnership though this form of partnership is only available for professional service providers such as law firms and accounting firms.

12. A limited partnership can be thought of as a hybrid between a private limited company and a general partnership.

13. In Hong Kong, a limited partnership must consist of one or more general partners and one or more limited partners. The general partner is

responsible for the management of the partnership and has unlimited personal liability for the liabilities of the partnership. The limited partner is not involved in the management of the partnership and, subject to certain exceptions, his or her liability is limited to the amount of his or her capital contribution to the partnership.

14. The main features of a limited partnership in the Mainland are similar to those of a limited partnership in Hong Kong.

## ▋ *Sole Proprietorship*

15. A Hong Kong sole proprietorship is an unincorporated business wholly and directly owned by an individual. It is not a separate legal entity. This means that the individual has unlimited personal liability for the liabilities of the business.

16. The main features of a sole proprietorship in the Mainland are similar to those of a sole proprietorship in Hong Kong.

## Private Company and LLC

17. The private company and the LLC are the most commonly used business vehicles both in Hong Kong and the Mainland. This section sets out in greater detail the following aspects of a private company and an LLC:

   (1) incorporation

   (2) share capital

   (3) corporate governance and

   (4) main reporting and filing requirements.

## ▋ *Incorporation*

18. Incorporating a private company in Hong Kong is a relatively straight forward and quick process. A private company may apply for incorporation by submitting the following documents to the Companies Registry:

   (1) the completed incorporation form (which contains information on particulars of director(s), secretary, shareholder(s), share capital, etc. of the private company)

(2) its articles of association

(3) the notice to Business Registration Office (which is an application for business registration) and

(4) the prescribed fees and levy.

19. Upon obtaining approval of an application for incorporation, the Companies Registry issues the Certificate of Incorporation certifying the date of incorporation and the Inland Revenue Department issues the Business Registration Certificate.

20. The approval process takes around four working days to complete.

21. In contrast, the process of establishing an LLC in the Mainland is slightly more complicated and time-consuming. An LLC may apply for incorporation by submitting the following to the local branch of the State Administration for Market Regulations (the "SAMR"):

(1) an application form

(2) the qualification documents of shareholder(s) and proof of identity of natural person shareholder(s)

(3) the documents on domicile or principal place of business

(4) its articles of association and

(5) other materials to be submitted as required by any laws or administrative regulations or the SAMR.

22. Upon granting approval of an application for registration of establishment, the local branch of the SAMR issues a business license to the LLC. The date of issuance of the business license is the date of establishment of the LLC. The approval time for the establishment procedure varies depending on the identity of the applicant. If the applicant is a resident of the Mainland, the establishment process usually takes one to two weeks to complete. If the applicant is a resident of Hong Kong, then the establishment of an LLC in the Mainland will be treated as a wholly foreign-owned enterprise and the establishment procedure may take several months to complete.

# ■ *Share Capital*

23. Unless a private company or an LLC operates in regulated industries (such as the banking or insurance industries), there is no prescribed minimum or maximum share capital requirement.

24. Shares of a private company may be issued for cash or non-cash assets (such as property). The position is similar for an LLC.

25. In Hong Kong, share capital may be divided into different classes of shares with special rights attached to them as prescribed by the articles of association of a private company but the position is somewhat uncertain in the context of an LLC in the Mainland.

# ■ *Corporate Governance*

Director

26. The general powers of managing a private company are usually vested in its directors.

27. A private company is required to appoint at least one director who is a natural person. There is no legal requirements on the maximum number of directors. Directors can be individuals (over 18 years old) or corporations of any nationality, domicile and residence.[2]

28. The duties that a director owes to a private company are derived from several sources including the Companies Ordinance (Cap.622) (the "Companies Ordinance"), the relevant case law and the articles of association of a private company. The broad principles of the duties imposed on directors are set out below:

    (1) a duty to act in good faith and for the benefit of the private company

    (2) a duty to use powers for proper purpose

    (3) a duty not to delegate powers except with proper authorisation and duty to exercise independent judgment

    (4) a duty to exercise reasonable care, skill and diligence

    (5) a duty to avoid conflicts between personal and company interests

    (6) a duty not to enter into transactions in which a director has an interest (unless in compliance with the law)

(7)   a duty not to gain advantage from use of position as a director

(8)   a duty of confidentiality and duty not to make unauthorised use of company information

(9)   a duty not to accept personal benefit from third parties conferred because of his/her position as a director

(10)  a duty to observe the private company's constitution (including its articles of association) and resolutions  and

(11)  a duty to keep proper books of account.

29.   An LLC is required to appoint at least one executive director.  The duties that a director owes to an LLC are derived from several sources including the Company Law of the People's Republic of China (the "PRC Company Law"), the relevant administrative regulations and the articles of association of the LLC.  The broad principles of the duties imposed on a director of an LLC are similar to those that apply to a director of a private company.

Shareholder

30.   A private company is required to have at least one registered shareholder whose name, address and shareholding are filed on public record at the Companies Registry.  Shareholders can be individuals or corporations.

31.   The shareholders' general powers to manage a private company are subject to the provisions of the Companies Ordinance, the circumstances prescribed by the relevant case law and the articles of association of the private company.  For example, the Companies Ordinance requires shareholders' approval for matters such as the following:

(1)   alteration to the articles of association

(2)   reduction in share capital

(3)   appointment and removal of auditors  and

(4)   appointment and removal of directors.

32. Similar to a private company, an LLC is required to have at least one shareholder. However, it is usual for LLCs to have two or more shareholders since additional rules apply to LLCs with only one shareholder. For example, if the sole shareholder cannot prove that the assets of an LLC are completely separate from those of the sole shareholder without intermeddling of, for instance, funds of the LLC, then the sole shareholder is jointly and severally liable for the liabilities of that LLC.

33. The shareholders' general powers to manage an LLC are subject to the provisions of the PRC Company Law and the articles of association of the LLC. The types of matters that require shareholders' approval under the PRC Company Law are similar to those under the Companies Ordinance.

Company Secretary

34. A private company must have a company secretary which is either another company with its registered office or place of business in Hong Kong or an individual ordinarily resident in Hong Kong.

35. If a private company has only one director, then the company secretary must not be the sole director or a body corporate whose sole director is also the sole director of the private company.

36. A company secretary's functions are to maintain the statutory books of a private company, including the registers of directors and shareholders, the minute book of directors' and shareholders' meetings and the share certificate book, and to prepare the documents which have to be filed on public record.

37. There is, however, no mandatory requirement in the Mainland for an LLC to appoint a company secretary.

Legal Representative

38. "Legal Representative" is a concept that exists under the PRC Company Law, but not under the Companies Ordinance. An LLC is required to appoint a legal representative. The legal representative is the principal representative of the LLC and has legal powers to represent and bind the LLC.

39. Only the chairman of a board of directors, the executive director or the manager of the LLC can act as the legal representative of the LLC.

## Supervisor

40. "Supervisor" is a concept that exists under the PRC Company Law, but not under the Companies Ordinance. An LLC is required to appoint at least one supervisor. The function of a supervisor is to supervise the directors and senior management personnel of the LLC. As such, the supervisor must not be a director or senior management personnel of the LLC.

# ▌ *Main Reporting and Filing Requirements*

41. A private company is required to comply with certain reporting and filing obligations in accordance with the Companies Ordinance. Likewise, an LLC is required to comply with certain reporting and filing obligations in accordance with the PRC Company Law. Some of the major reporting and filing requirements are set out below in this section.

## Financial Statements

42. A private company is required to keep proper books of accounts. Its accounts must be audited every year. The audited financial statements must be submitted to the Hong Kong Inland Revenue Department and presented to the shareholders at the annual general meeting.

43. Similarly, an LLC is required to keep proper books of accounts which must be audited every year. The audited financial statements must be delivered to the shareholders within the time limit as prescribed by its articles of association.

## Books and Registers

44. A private company is required to keep certain books and registers such as:

(1) a register of shareholders, which records the particulars of each shareholder of the company since its incorporation and details of the respective shareholdings

(2) a register of directors, which records the particulars of each director of the company since its incorporation

(3) a register of company secretaries, which records the particulars of each secretary of the company since its incorporation

(4) a register of charges, which records the particulars of every charge affecting the company's property or undertaking

(5) a set of minutes book of all directors' and shareholders' meetings, which include all resolutions passed by the directors and shareholders of the company and

(6) a register of significant controllers, which records the particulars of each significant controller of the company (as defined under the Companies Ordinance).

45. In the Mainland, an LLC is required to keep a register of shareholders and a record of the names of all shareholders with the SAMR.

Annual Return and Notification of Changes

46. A private company is required to file its annual returns with the Companies Registry on an annual basis. The annual returns show the updated particulars of a company's share capital, shareholders, directors and registered charges.

47. Further, a private company is required to notify the Companies Registry and an LLC is required to notify the SAMR within a prescribed period after changes such as those mentioned below are made:

(1) any change of company name

(2) any change to the articles of association

(3) any change of directors or company secretary (or any change in the filed particulars of any existing directors or company secretary)

(4) change of address of the registered office and

(5) any allotment of shares.

## Shareholders' Agreement

48. A shareholders' agreement is a key legal document that regulates the affairs of the company.

49. The main purposes of the shareholders' agreement are:

(1)   from the viewpoint of the founders of a start-up that is about to enter its fundraising phase, to set out the duties and obligations of the founders and the investors vis-à-vis each other  and

(2)   from the viewpoint of the investors who are looking to invest into a start-up company, to ensure business stability through the terms of the shareholders' agreement.

<u>Board Representation</u>

50.  Generally speaking, investors want to have some form of board representation so that they can have a say in the company's operations.

51.  On the other hand, founders want to ensure that they maintain sufficient control of the board. Accordingly, the shareholders' agreement may empower the founders to appoint and remove directors from the board, and investors holding a certain percentage of shares to hold the right to appoint a director.

<u>Reserved Matters</u>

52.  Investors may ask for certain decisions of the company to require the unanimous consent of all shareholders before the same can be passed as resolutions, such as allotment of shares, variation of the company's capital structure and amendment of the company's constitution.

53.  This mechanism enables the investors as minority shareholders to have a say in major decisions of the corporation.

54.  From the perspective of the founders, care should be given to consider if the reserved matters clause would hamper the founders' ability to make swift decisions regarding the day-to-day operations of the company.

<u>Restrictions on Share Transfer</u>

55.  From the perspective of the founders, a shareholders' agreement should contain restrictions on share transfer. The most common type of restriction is the right of first refusal by which a shareholder, if he or she wishes to sell the shares to a third party, he or she must first offer these shares for sale to the other shareholders on the same terms and conditions. If the offer is not accepted, the shareholder can then sell the shares to the third party.

## Drag-along Rights

56. This right is to ensure that when a founder decides to sell the start-up, he or she will be able to procure all the other shareholders to sell their shares to the same third-party buyer as well.

57. From the perspective of the founders, it provides flexibility and an easy exit route by eliminating the risk of a difficult minority shareholder from blocking the sale of the start-up.

58. From the perspective of the investors, it ensures that they will be treated on the same footing during the exit.

---

[2] No corporate director is allowed in the case of a private company which is a member of a group of companies of which a listed company is a member.

# 02 Employment

## General

1.  Employment in Hong Kong is less regulated than many other jurisdictions, such as the Mainland (including the Greater Bay Area), the European Union and the United States. The primary piece of legislation, the Employment Ordinance (the "EO"), prescribes certain basic rights and protection for most employees and applies equally to every employee engaged under a contract of employment in Hong Kong with only a few minor exceptions.

2.  Generally speaking, a contract of employment governs the relationship between an employer and an employee. Any term or condition of a contract of employment that seeks to reduce any right, benefit or protection conferred upon an employee by the EO will be void. So, to the extent that any contractual terms are less favourable, the EO will prevail.

3.  In the Mainland, the primary pieces of employment-related legislation are the PRC Labour Law and the PRC Labour Contract Law ("LCL"). There are also specific laws (and in some cases, city-specific regulations) around mediation and arbitration of labour dispute, social insurance contributions, labour dispatch, etc.

## Right to Work [3]

4.  An employer must ensure that its employees have a right to work in Hong Kong. In general, unless a person has the right of abode or right to

land in the HKSAR, that person will require an appropriate visa to work in Hong Kong. The sponsor of an employment visa would typically be the employer who is responsible for repatriation of the employee upon the expiration of his or her permitted stay in Hong Kong.

5.   Hong Kong residents are not required to apply for work permits to work in the Mainland, they can use their "Residence Permit for Hong Kong, Macao and Taiwan Residents" or the "Mainland Travel Permit for Hong Kong and Macao Resident" as valid identity documents. For those without a "Residence Permit for Hong Kong, Macao and Taiwan Residents" or the "Mainland Travel Permit for Hong Kong and Macao Resident", a work visa (Z Visa) and a residence permit are required.

## Independent Contractor vs Employee

6.   It is always important to determine whether a worker is an employee or an independent contractor because an independent contractor does not get the same level of benefits and protections afforded to any employee such as those prescribed in the EO. The modern approach is to examine all the features of the parties' relationship against a list of factors and decide whether the relationship is, as a matter of overall impression, one of employment (and the label given to it by the parties is not conclusive and often carries little weight).

7.   The Court has taken into account factors such as (this is not an exhaustive list and the importance of each factor depends on the situation): the degree of control an employer has over the individual, the employer's obligation to provide work and the individual's obligation to accept work, whether the individual has to provide his or her own tools and equipment etc.

## Employee's Benefits and Entitlements

### ▌ *Form of Contract* [4]

8.   Unlike the Mainland, there is no requirement in Hong Kong for a contract of employment to be in writing. However, upon the written request by an employee before the commencement of employment, the employer must give written particulars of certain conditions of employment. Where the contract of employment is in writing, the employer must provide a copy of it to the employee immediately after it is signed. The basic conditions required to be stated are the wages and wage period, the amount of end-of-year payment (if any) or its proportional entitlement

and the length of notice required to terminate the employment.

9. In the Mainland, the labour contract (which is the equivalent of a contract of employment in Hong Kong) must be executed by the parties in writing (except for certain part-time employees), failure to do so will result in a penalty against the employer. The basic conditions mentioned in the preceding paragraph can either be incorporated in the labour contract itself or by way of an employee handbook which the labour contract can incorporate by reference.

## ▌ *Wages* [5]

10. Subject to certain exceptions, an employer must pay employees the statutory minimum wage. As of 1 May 2023, the statutory minimum wage rate has been increased to HK$40 per hour.

11. In the Mainland, the minimum wage level varies from city to city and may be different for full-time employees and part-time employees, depending on the city.

## ▌ *Hours* [6]

12. Except in relation to employment of young persons in industrial undertakings, where special regulations apply, there are no statutory provisions which prescribe a maximum number of working hours. The EO does, however, provide that in addition to paid statutory (public) holidays, an employee is entitled to not less than one rest day in every period of seven days.

13. In the Mainland, an employee's standard working hours should not be more than 8 hours per day, 44 hours per week and there should at least be one rest day per week (i.e. respectively "Standard Working Hours Scheme"). Overtime pay should be paid outside the Standard Working Hours Scheme depending on whether the additional hours worked take place on a work day, a rest day or a statutory holiday at the rates of 150%, 200% and 300% respectively. Subject to the approval of the relevant labour authority, an employee may also be working under a "Flexible Working Hours Scheme" or a "Comprehensive Calculation Working Hours Scheme".

## *Annual Leave* [7]

14. Employees are entitled to a minimum of between 7 and 14 days annual leave for each period of 12 months employment, calculated on the basis of the length of service.

15. In the Mainland, employees who have worked for a continuous period of 12 months (with any employer) are entitled to a minimum of between 5 and 15 days annual leave for each calendar year, calculated also on the basis of the aggregate length of service with any employer whether current or past.

## *Sick Leave* [8]

16. An employee is entitled to paid sick leave at the rate of four-fifths of the employee's daily average wages. Entitlement to sick leave may be accumulated at the rate of 2 paid sickness days for each completed month of continuous employment during the first 12 months of employment and at the rate of 4 paid sickness days for each month after that, up to a maximum of 120 paid sickness days. The entitlement to sickness allowance with the exception of maternity related sickness only applies, however, to periods of absence due to sickness of more than 4 consecutive days.

17. In the Mainland, an employee's entitlement to sick leave depends on whether the sickness or injury is work-related. In respect of a work-related sickness or injury, an employee is generally entitled to a maximum of 12 months' of sick leave with full pay, subject to the production of the requisite medical certificate. In respect of a non-work-related sickness or injury, the law is silent on the maximum number of days of sick leave but an employee is entitled to a "medical treatment period" in respect of the sickness or injury, which ranges from 3 to 24 months depending on the employee's length of service (with any employer). The amount of pay during the "medical treatment period" must not be less than 80% of the applicable minimum wage (though this rate may vary between cities) and an employer cannot unilaterally terminate the employee during that period.

## *Maternity and Paternity Leave* [9]

18. Subject to certain eligibility requirements under the EO, female employees are entitled to paid maternity leave of 14 weeks (increased from 10 weeks to 14 weeks with effect from 11 December 2020) or as

provided by the terms of the employment, whichever is more favourable. Maternity leave pay is paid at the rate of four-fifths of the employee's daily average wages. The government will reimburse an employer for payment of additional maternity leave pay in respect of the additional 4 weeks under the 2020 amendment, which is capped at HK$80,000.

19. Subject to certain eligibility requirements under the EO, a male employee is entitled to paid paternity leave of five working days at the rate of four-fifths of the employee's daily average wages for each confinement of their spouse/partner.

20. In the Mainland, a female employee is entitled to 98 days of maternity leave in total in respect of her first child, including 15 days of maternity leave prior to the expected date. An additional 15 days of maternity leave is granted if the employee experiences a difficult childbirth or gives birth to more than one child during a single period of delivery. The entitlement to maternity leave may vary across different local rules. An employer must pay a female employee not less than her normal salary during her maternity leave.

21. Further, a male employee is entitled to paternity leave ranging from 7 to 30 days depending on the local rules of the locality in the Mainland, provided that the employee's wife gives birth to her first child. An employer must pay a male employee not less than his normal salary during his paternity leave.

## ▌ *MPF, Retirement and Social Insurance Scheme* [10]

22. Every employer in Hong Kong is required to contribute an amount equal to at least 5% of an employee's monthly salary (capped at HK$1,500) to a retirement scheme that is registered as an MPF scheme. Every employee is also required to contribute at least 5% of their monthly salary (also capped at HK$1,500) to the scheme. There are, however, certain exceptions to this general rule.

23. In the Mainland, social insurance contributions comprising the basic endowment insurance, basic medical insurance, unemployment insurance, employment injury insurance, maternity insurance and the housing fund are required to be made on a monthly basis by both the employer and the employee. The total amount of the employer's contribution and employee's contribution are prescribed by the city in which the labour relationship exists, which is generally a percentage of the employee's monthly wages. The total amount of the employer's

and employee's contributions are made at a prescribed percentage of the employee's monthly salary (where the employer's contributions are generally higher than the employee's contributions but both subject to a cap at three times the local average monthly salary during the previous year).

## ▌ *Workers' Compensation* [11]

24. An employer must maintain insurance coverage in case of work-related injuries but, otherwise, there is no statutory requirement to provide medical benefits.

25. There is no additional compulsory insurance coverage in the Mainland other than the social insurance contributions made as mentioned in paragraph 23 above.

## ▌ *Severance Pay and Long Service Pay* [12]

26. An employee who has been continuously employed for not less than 24 months is entitled to statutory severance pay if he or she is dismissed by reason of redundancy or if the employee is laid off. Employees who have been employed under a continuous contract for not less than 5 years are entitled to long service pay on termination (other than summary dismissal for misconduct).

27. The right to severance pay and the right to long service pay are mutually exclusive. The amount of severance/long service pay is two-thirds of a month's pay for each year of employment or two-thirds of HK$22,500 (i.e., HK$15,000), whichever is less, up to a maximum payment of HK$390,000. The amount of any contractual gratuity based on length of service covering the same period is deductible from the amount of severance/long service pay due to an employee. In addition, an employer has the statutory right to reduce its severance pay or long service pay payable to an employee by offsetting its contributions to the MPF or retirement scheme in respect of that employee (however this offsetting mechanism will be abolished with effect from 1 May 2025, following which benefits derived from employer's mandatory MPF contributions will no longer be capable of being used to offset against the severance pay or long service pay payable to an employee).

28. In the Mainland, severance pay is known as "statutory economic compensation". An employer is generally required to pay economic

compensation upon termination of the labour relationship if:

(1)  the employer's proposed termination is agreed to by the employee (i.e. a mutually agreed termination initiated by the employer)

(2)  the labour relationship is terminated by the employer unilaterally (unless the termination is based on one of the grounds listed in Article 39 of the LCL such as the employee's serious misconduct ── see "Termination" below)

(3)  the employee resigns as a result of the employer's failure to comply with certain material obligations listed in Article 38 of the LCL e.g. failure to pay remuneration (see "Termination" below)

(4)  the labour relationship is terminated upon the expiry of a fixed-term labour contract (unless the employee refuses an offer of contract renewal on terms similar  to or better than those contained in the previous fixed term labour contract)

(5)  the employment is terminated on the employer's bankruptcy, revocation of employer's business licence, or the employer has been ordered to close down / deregister or has opted for voluntary liquidation.

## ▌ *Termination* [13]

29.  A contract of employment may be terminated by notice or by payment in lieu of notice by the employer or the employee. The payment of wages in lieu of notice must be calculated in accordance with the EO. In exceptional circumstances, an employer may summarily dismiss an employee (without notice or payment in lieu) on any of the statutory grounds laid down in section 9 of the EO, e.g. where an employee is guilty of fraud or dishonesty.

30.  An employee on probation may be terminated without notice during the first month of the probation period and by not less than 7 days' notice after the first month of the probation period. After the probation period or if there is no probation period, unless summarily dismissed, an employee is entitled to the agreed period of notice with the employer under the employment contract but not less than 7 days. The length of notice excludes annual leave and maternity leave.

31. It is unlawful to terminate the employment of an employee when the employee is, among other things, on sick leave and receiving statutory sickness allowance, pregnant, entitled to statutory employees' compensation before certain certificates are issued by the Labour Department. It is also unlawful to terminate an employee due to any unlawful discriminatory reasons (see below).

32. In the Mainland, there are two common types of labour contract:

   (1) a fixed term labour contract (which can cover a period as agreed between the employer and employee) and

   (2) an indefinite labour contract (which provides for an indefinite period).

33. An employer is required to enter into an indefinite contract with an employee if:

   (1) the employee has worked for the employer for a year without a written contract

   (2) the employee has completed two prior fixed-term contracts with the employer or

   (3) a request is made by the employee who has worked for the employer for 10 years or more.

34. A labour contract may be terminated by:

   (1) the mutual agreement of the parties pursuant to Article 36 of the LCL

   (2) an employee upon giving 30 days' notice (or 3 days' notice during probation) or payment in lieu of notice pursuant to Article 37 of LCL for any reason

   (3) an employee with immediate effect pursuant to Article 38 of the LCL if the employer fails to comply with certain material obligations, e.g. failure to pay remuneration

   (4) an employer with immediate effect on any of the statutory grounds set out in Article 39 of the LCL, e.g. where the employee seriously violates the rules and regulations of the employer

   (5) an employer with 30 days' notice (or 3 days' notice during

probation) or payment in lieu of notice on any of the no-fault grounds set out in Article 40 of the LCL, e.g. where the employee is incompetent to perform his or her duties and remains so after training  or

(6)   an employer by reason of redundancy pursuant to Article 41 of the LCL.

## ▌ *Right against Unlawful Discrimination and Harassment* [14]

35.   Discrimination on the grounds of sex, pregnancy, breastfeeding, marital status, disability, family status and race is currently prohibited under the anti-discrimination ordinances in Hong Kong. There is no specific protection against discrimination on the basis of age or sexual orientation nor is there any equal pay legislation in Hong Kong.

36.   It is unlawful for an employer to discriminate against an employee on a prohibited ground:

(1)   in the way the employer affords the employee access to opportunities for promotion, transfer or training, or to any other benefits, services or facilities

(2)   by refusing or deliberately omitting to afford the employee access to such opportunities, or to any other benefits, services or facilities which by the terms of employment the employer affords the employee or

(3)   by dismissing the employee, or subjecting the employee to any other detriment or unwelcome conduct.

37.   Harassment on the ground of sex, breastfeeding, disability and race is also prohibited under the Hong Kong anti-discrimination ordinances. Unlawful harassment occurs where a person makes an unwelcomed conduct towards another individual on one of the prohibited grounds and may take different forms, e.g. making  inappropriate or offensive comments or jokes, and such conduct may be one-off or consist of repeated actions.

38.   In the Mainland, this topic is still a developing area of law but in principle, discrimination on the grounds of nationality, race, gender, religious relief, disability, residence status (i.e. rural or urban worker), or physical status (e.g. a carrier of epidemic pathogens such as hepatitis B) are prohibited. The newly introduced PRC Civil Code also expressly

prohibits sexual harassment and establishes a civil liability framework to hold offenders accountable. An employer must therefore prevent sexual harassment of female employees in their workplaces (including to provide training and adopt reasonable measures for investigation of sexual harassment complaints).

# Employer's Tax Obligations [15]

39. Generally speaking, an employer in Hong Kong is under an obligation to keep employees' payroll record and report any changes of employees' particulars to the Inland Revenue Department ("IRD"). If an employer receives an Employer's Return (BIR56A), the employer must complete it and lodge it with IRD within one month.

40. An employer in Hong Kong is not required to withhold tax for employees. However, if an employee intends to leave Hong Kong for over one month following cessation of employment, the employer is required to notify the IRD of the impending departure and must temporarily withhold all payment due to the employee until one month from the date of notification or until receipt of the "Letter of Release" issued by the IRD, whichever is earlier.

41. In the Mainland, some tax filing obligations fall on both the employer and the employee. Generally speaking, an employer must withhold individual income tax from the income payable to an employee in accordance with the PRC Individual Income Tax Law but failure to do so will not absolve the liability of the employee to pay his or her tax.

---

[3] Immigration Ordinance (Cap. 115)
[4] Employment Ordinance (Cap. 57)；PRC Labour Contract Law
[5] Minimum Wage Ordinance (Cap. 608)；PRC Labour Law；PRC Labour Contract Law
[6] Employment Ordinance (Cap. 57)；PRC Labour Law
[7] Employment Ordinance (Cap. 57)；PRC Labour Law；PRC Regulation on Paid Annual Leave for Employees
[8] Employment Ordinance (Cap. 57)；PRC Regulation on Work-Related Injury Insurance (2010 Revision)；PRC Labour Law；PRC Provisions on Period of Medical Treatment for Illness or for Non-Work-Related Injury Incurred by Enterprise Employees 1994；Opinions on Several Issues Concerning the Implementation of PRC Labour Law
[9] Employment Ordinance (Cap. 57)；PRC Special Rules on the Labour Protection of Female Employees；PRC Labour Law
[10] Mandatory Provident Fund Schemes Ordinance (Cap. 485)；PRC Social Insurance Law
[11] Employees' Compensation Ordinance (Cap. 282)；PRC Regulations on Work-Related Injury Insurance
[12] Employment Ordinance (Cap. 57)；Employment & Retirement Schemes Legislation (Offsetting Arrangement) (Amendment) Bill 2022；PRC Labour Law；PRC Labour Contract Law
[13] Employment Ordinance (Cap. 57)；Employees' Compensation Ordinance (Cap. 282)；PRC Labour Contract Law
[14] Employment Ordinance (Cap. 57)；Sex Discrimination Ordinance (Cap. 480)；Disability Discrimination Ordinance (Cap. 487)；Family Status Discrimination Ordinance (Cap. 527)；Race Discrimination Ordinance (Cap. 602)；PRC Labour Law；PRC Employment Promotion Law；PRC Special Rules on the Labour Protection of Female Employees, PRC Civil Code
[15] Inland Revenue Ordinance (Cap. 112)；PRC Individual Income Tax Law (2018 Amendment)

# Intellectual Property ("IP") Rights

**namely Copyright, Trade Mark, Patent, and Registered Designs**

## General

1. Works and inventions may be protected by different categories of IP rights, namely copyright, trade mark, patent, and registered designs.

2. IP rights are territorial and may or may not require registration. Where registration is needed, the application requires careful drafting (especially for patent) and one should engage a lawyer to guide through the application process.

3. IP rights registered in Hong Kong are not automatically protected in the Mainland, and vice-versa. In order to obtain protection in Hong Kong, the Mainland and any other jurisdictions, registration must be done in each jurisdiction separately. Traders should prioritise registration in their most important markets, their place of research and development, and their place of manufacturing (if any).

4. It may constitute infringement if one copies or uses the IP rights of others in goods or services or for his or her business. The infringement act may attract civil or even criminal liability.

# Categories of IP

## ▌ *Copyright* [16]

5. Copyright protects the expression of ideas (but not the ideas themselves) in specified categories of work: literary works, dramatic works, musical works, artistic works, sound recordings, films, broadcasts, cable programmes, and typographical arrangements of published edition. A work may be protected by more than one category of copyright.

6. In both Hong Kong and the Mainland, copyright arises automatically if the work is original and recorded in material form. A piece of work is considered "original" if it originates from the author, and results from his or her skill, labour and effort.

7. Generally speaking, the author is the first owner of copyright in a piece of work. Special rules apply to works created by employees or an independent contractor on one's commission i.e. the commissioned works as follows:

   (1) In Hong Kong, for works created by an employee within his or her normal duties of employment, the copyright in the work belongs to the employer, unless there is an agreement to the contrary. In the Mainland, the position is different and unless there is an agreement to the contrary, the employee generally owns the copyright in the work but the employer has certain rights to enjoy the work.

   (2) Under both Hong Kong and PRC law, ownership of copyright in commissioned works is determined by an agreement with the independent contractor. If there is no agreement, or if the agreement does not mention this, then copyright will belong to the independent contractor by default as the author.

8. There is no registration system for copyright in Hong Kong. However, copyright registration in the Mainland is optional but generally recommended as it serves as *prima facie* proof of ownership in case of dispute.

9. Generally speaking, copyright lasts for the life span of the author plus 50 years but different terms of protection may apply to various categories of copyright work.

## ▌ *Trade mark* [17]

10. A trade mark is any mark (such as a word or logo or a combination of both)

which is capable of associating goods or services to one particular trader. If a trade mark is registered, the owner can enjoy stronger protection against infringement under statute  otherwise, the unregistered trade mark can still be protected by the common law action of passing-off.

11. To obtain registration, a trade mark must be distinctive and non-descriptive, and not be identical or confusingly similar to prior trademarks registered in the relevant territory. The registration should cover the goods and services currently offered and may be offered in the near future.

12. A trade mark registration is valid for 10 years from the date of registration, which can be continuously renewed.

13. When designing a new name, logo or product etc., a trader may conduct online searches in respect of official databases in Hong Kong and in the Mainland to see if other traders may already be using the same or similar name or idea, or have obtained corresponding registration.

## ▌ Patent [18]

14. An invention can be protected by patent if the invention is:

    (1)  new —— meaning not known to anyone before the application is filed

    (2)  involves an inventive step —— meaning it is not obvious  and

    (3)  is susceptible of industrial application —— meaning it can be made or used in any kind of industry.

15. Registration is required and the term of protection depends on the type of patent obtained and the place of registration (generally with a maximum of 20 years except for short-term patent of 8 years in Hong Kong and utility model patent of 10 years in the Mainland).

16. Where an invention is made or developed partially or entirely in the Mainland, a trader should first consider which jurisdiction(s) he or she would like to obtain patent protection for the invention (see paragraph 3 above):

    (1)  If patent protection in the Mainland is desired, then a trader can simply file a patent application in the Mainland.

    (2)  If patent protection outside the Mainland is desired, then a trader should first obtain a foreign filing licence from the PRC National Intellectual Property Administration before filing a patent application for the invention

in the relevant foreign jurisdiction. If this is not done and when the trader subsequently files a patent application for the invention in the Mainland, then approval for the Mainland application may not be granted.[19]

17. Where an invention is made or developed partially or entirely in Hong Kong, a trader can simply file a patent application for the invention in the relevant foreign jurisdiction outside Hong Kong as the notion of a foreign filing licence has no application in Hong Kong.

## ▌ *Registered designs* [20]

18. A registered design protects the appearance of a finished product, e.g. fabric pattern, jewellery design, or product packaging design.

19. Registration is required and the maximum period of registration is 25 years in Hong Kong and 15 years in the Mainland.

## ▌ *Infringement*

20. An infringement can occur if one copies or uses the IP rights of others in goods or services or for his or her business e.g. in promotional materials.

21. There are a number of defences available to an infringement claim e.g. incidental inclusion of copyright work, or using a registered trade mark to refer to the goods or services for which the mark is registered.

22. An infringement may incur civil or even criminal liability, depending on the types of IP right infringed and the infringing act being alleged by the owner.

23. There is also a common law action known as passing-off, which protects a trader's goodwill and reputation. An action of passing off occurs when a trader unlawfully misrepresents that his or her goods or services are those of another trader. There is a similar cause of action known as "unfair competition" in the Mainland.[21]

24. In a civil claim, the remedies for infringement and passing-off are by and large similar in Hong Kong and the Mainland and both may include an injunction to stop the infringing act, a declaration for infringement, damages or account of profits, recovery of reasonable legal costs and/or delivery-up or destruction of the infringing materials.

---

16  Copyright Ordinance (Cap. 528) ； PRC Copyright Law
17  Trade Marks Ordinance (Cap. 559) ； PRC Trade Mark Law
18  Patents Ordinance (Cap. 514) ； PRC Patent Law
19  Article 19, PRC Patent Law
20  Registered Designs Ordinance (Cap. 522) ； PRC Patent Law
21  PRC Anti-Unfair Competition Law

04

# Types of Fund Raising

## General

1. Raising funds is one of the most important first steps for any new business. As the business grows, the financing requirements of the business may also develop. This Chapter provides an overview of the financing options available to start-ups in Hong Kong and the key issues to consider when start-ups apply for loans.

2. In general, the options for business to raise funds can be divided into two major categories: debt financing and equity financing. Debt financing involves the borrowing of money with an obligation to repay it, while equity financing involves taking money in exchange for giving a portion of the ownership of the company to the investor. Each of the two forms of financing has its pros and cons. The key advantage of debt financing is that the owner gives up less control of the business, while the key advantage of equity financing is that there is no obligation to repay the funds or to pay any interest or fee charged for the funding.

3. In addition to private funding, start-ups may also benefit from the funding schemes offered by the Government and other public bodies to promote entrepreneurship and support small businesses.

# Major Types of Financing Options for Start-ups

## ▌ *Funding schemes offered by the Government and other organisations*

4.  Under the Government's Youth Development Fund, the Funding Scheme for Youth Entrepreneurship in the Guangdong-Hong Kong-Macao Greater Bay Area subsidises Hong Kong Non-Governmental Organisations to provide start-up assistance to young people who start their businesses in Hong Kong and the Greater Bay Area. It provides youth start-ups with seed funding of up to HK$600,000 through subsidising funded organisations in the form of a matching fund.

5.  Funding may also be available from specific schemes offered by other government departments, local universities and non-profit organisations. Some of the programmes are geared towards start-ups in the technology area. These include:

    (1)  Cyberport Creative Micro Fund offered by Cyberport

    (2)  Innovation and Technology Venture Fund offered by the Government

    (3)  Ideation Programme offered by The Hong Kong Science & Technology Parks

    (4)  Technology Start-up Support Scheme for Universities offered by the Government

    (5)  Youth Business Hong Kong by The Hong Kong Federation of Youth Groups.

6.  Apart from grants, these schemes often include mentoring, professional consultation, co-working space and other assistance to start-ups.

7.  The criteria, requirements, application procedure and vetting process for these programmes vary. Start-ups should refer to the website of the relevant scheme to obtain further information.

## ▌ *Investment*

8.  **Seed round:** The earliest funds for a start-up often come from the personal savings of the owner or family and friends.

9.  **Angel round:** In the next stage, the start-up may have developed a prototype and a business model. Start-ups may then seek investment from angel investors, who are often wealthy entrepreneurs, in exchange for equity or convertible debt. Apart from working capital, angel investors can also benefit start-ups with their business network, connections and experience. Please refer to paragraphs 11 to 15 of Chapter VI for more information on legal and regulatory issues relating to angel investors.

10. **Series A round**: As a start-up continues to develop, it may attract institutional investment from venture capital. Venture capitalists typically obtain shares in a start-up in return for its investment. The goal of their investment is to generate profits through an "exit" event, such as the initial public offering (IPO) of the company or the sale of the shares in a merger and acquisition (M&A) transaction. Series A round may be followed by subsequent rounds (i.e. Series B, Series C, etc.).

## ▌ *Crowdfunding*

11. Crowdfunding means raising funds online by asking for small amounts of money from a large number of people. It may be conducted through commercially-operated online platforms. Please refer to paragraphs 11 to 19 of Chapter VI for more information on the legal and regulatory issues relating to crowdfunding.

## ▌ *Loans*

12. Start-ups can also consider loans from financial institutions (e.g. licensed banks) and other sources. As banks usually assess the past performance of a business when approving loan applications, bank loans are more appropriate for start-ups with an established track record.

## Overview of Loan Financing

## ▌ *Loans from financial institutions*

13. If a start-up would like to obtain a loan from a financial institution to fund its business-related expenses, it can consider applying for a business loan. Financial institutions will assess the credit of a start-up before deciding whether to approve the loan.

14. Alternatively, it is also possible for an individual (e.g. the owner of a start-up business) to take out a personal loan from a financial institution and then invest the proceeds in the start-up. The procedure and requirements for applying for personal loans are usually simpler. However, lenders will likely assess the income and credit score of the individual before approving the loan application. In considering whether a start-up or an owner should apply for a loan to fund the expenses of the business, start-up owners should also consider how personal funds and the business' funds are separated.

15. Start-ups can also consider if they are eligible to participate in the SME Financing Guarantee Scheme offered by HKMC Insurance Limited (a wholly-owned subsidiary of The Hong Kong Mortgage Corporation Limited). This scheme helps local SMEs obtain financing from participating financial institutions for meeting the SMEs' business needs by providing guarantee coverage for loan facilities.

16. Apart from the SME Financing Guarantee Scheme, some financial institutions also offer designated loan products which provide preferential terms for borrowers in the digital, innovation and technology sectors to support their development.

## ▌ *Applying for a loan and related documentation*

17. The requirements for applying for a loan vary. In addition to its application form, a lender usually requests a start-up to submit the following documents and information for the purpose of approving the application:

    (1)  business plan

    (2)  financial and bank statements

    (3)  financial information and identity documents of the business owner

    (4)  credit history

    (5)  details of any other investment or funding obtained by the business and

    (6)  (if a company is applying for the loan) constitutional documents of the company (e.g. certificate of incorporation, articles of association, register of directors, register of members, business registration certificate) and organisation chart.

18. After the loan is approved:

(1) the lender will sign a loan agreement with the borrower which sets out the terms and conditions on which the loan facility is provided and

(2) the lender may also require a start-up to sign certain corporate authorisation documents (e.g. board resolutions) to formally approve the borrower's entry into the loan transaction.

## ▌ *Terms of a loan*

19. Start-ups should carefully review the loan documentation prepared by the lender and consider if the terms are appropriate. The actual terms of a loan facility offered by each lender are likely to differ. Typically, a loan agreement will include the following key terms:

(1) Repayment: Whether the loan is repayable upon the lender's demand (i.e. an uncommitted facility), by instalments at regular specified intervals or in one lump sum at the end of the loan period.

(2) Interest and fees: As a return for making available a loan, a financial institution will charge interest on the amount borrowed, which could be either a fixed rate or a floating rate (e.g. based on the relevant bank's prime lending rate). In Hong Kong, it is illegal for any person to lend money at an effective interest rate above 48% per annum, while an effective interest rate exceeding 36% per annum is presumed to be extortionate unless proven otherwise.[22] Default interest may accrue for any overdue payment. In addition, the lender may charge an upfront or administration fee for providing the loan, which may be calculated at a percentage of the loan amount or on a fixed fee basis.

(3) Representations and undertakings: A representation is an assertion that a statement is factually true on the date that statement is made, whereas an undertaking is a promise to do something or to refrain from doing something. The representations in a loan agreement may relate to the capacity, ownership and financial condition of the borrower, the borrower's compliance with applicable laws, the accuracy and completeness of the financial information provided, etc. The undertakings in a loan agreement may also relate to those matters and, in addition, the restrictions on the creation of security over or the disposal of the borrower's assets, the provision of financial information, etc.

20. Under a committed facility, the lender may only demand the loan to be repaid before its due date(s) upon the occurrence of an event of default (for example, a representation being untrue or an undertaking having been breached) or any other specific event. Under an uncommitted facility, the lender has an overriding right to demand immediate repayment of the loan at any time, even if the borrower has not defaulted under the financing transaction. Naturally, an uncommitted facility poses more risk to a start-up as an unexpected demand from the lender can cause serious disruption to the business of a start-up. In return, lenders usually charge a lower interest rate for uncommitted facilities.

## ▌ *Guarantee and security*

21. Depending on a lender's assessment of the credit-worthiness of the business and its owner, as well as the availability of assets to support a borrower's repayment obligation, the lender may require the owner to guarantee the borrower's repayment of the loan or to provide assets of the business or its owner as security.

22. If the borrower fails to punctually repay the loan, the lender may:

    (1)  require the guarantor to pay the overdue amount owed by the borrower upon the lender's demand  and

    (2)  enforce any security provided and sell or otherwise deal with the security assets to repay the loan.

    Accordingly, a start-up should carefully consider the risks of guaranteeing a loan obtained by the business and providing security to support the loan, and obtain legal advice on their implications.

23. If:

    (1)  the security is provided by a company incorporated in Hong Kong or a registered non-Hong Kong company  and

    (2)  the security asset falls into one of the registrable categories identified in the Companies Ordinance (Cap. 622) (and, in the case of a registered non-Hong Kong company, the security asset is in Hong Kong),

    then the security document must be registered with the Hong Kong Companies Registry.

24. A certified copy of the instrument creating or evidencing the security over the asset, together with a statement of the particulars of that security in the specified form, must be submitted to the Hong Kong Companies Registry for registration within one month after the date of creation of the security against the company. If a company fails to deliver a statement of the particulars of specified charges as required, the company and every responsible person of the company will be liable to prosecution and fines.[23]

25. In addition to the registration requirement at the Hong Kong Companies Registry, if security is created over certain types of assets located or registered in Hong Kong, additional perfection, protection and/ or priority steps are also necessary or desirable from the lender's perspective. For example:

    (1) if security is created over real estate in Hong Kong, a lender would typically require registration of the security at the Hong Kong Land Registry and

    (2) if security is created over trade marks, patent or registered design registered in Hong Kong, a lender may require registration at the applicable register of the Hong Kong Intellectual Property Department.

26. In the Mainland, the applicable registration requirements depend on the type of assets over which security is created. For example:

    (1) if a pledge is created over equity interests in a limited liability company incorporated in the Mainland or shares in an unlisted company limited by shares incorporated in the Mainland, then the pledge should be registered with the local branch of the SAMR with which the subject company is incorporated or registered and

    (2) if a mortgage is created over real estate located in the Mainland, then the mortgage should be registered with the local real estate registry.

27. Start-ups should check the regulations and practice of the local authority handling the relevant registration before agreeing to provide security over assets in the Mainland to ensure compliance with the applicable laws and the prevailing local practices.

---

[22] Money Lenders Ordinance (Cap. 163) as amended with effect from 30 December 2022.
[23] Section 334, 335, 336 and 337 of the Companies Ordinance (Cap. 622)

# Social Venture Funding

## through Angel Investors and Crowdfunding

**05**

## General

1. Start-ups often face challenges in raising funds through the traditional channels (e.g. through bank loans or initial public offer) due to lack of proven track record. Angel investors and crowdfunding are two alternatives available to start-ups. This Chapter discusses the major legal and regulatory matters that start-ups should take note in deciding whether these alternatives are suitable to them.

## Ways of Raising Funds for Business

### ▌ *What are Angel Investors?*

2. The term "angel investors" typically refers to wealthy individuals who provide a one-time investment of capital to start-ups which they see potential for success, in exchange for equity (i.e. shares issued by the start-up company) or convertible debt (i.e. a debt which gives the investor a right to require the start-up company to repay the indebtedness with shares). The ultimate goal of angel investors is to realise their investment return by disposing of their shares of the start-up company after the start-up's business takes off and becomes profitable.

3. Angel investors are typically entrepreneurs themselves. In addition to

providing a source of funds to help a start-up in the early stages of its existence, angel investors are often prepared to share experience with and provide valuable guidance to start-ups.

4. An angel investor may be connected with the start-up's founders —— e.g. family and friends. Other sources of angel investors include referrals (whether formal or informal), conferences and events for start-ups and investors, or submissions of business plans and pitches.

## ▌ *What is Crowdfunding?*

5. In the context of start-ups, the term "crowdfunding" refers to the use of small amounts of money, obtained from a large number of persons (whether individuals or organizations), to fund a start-up's business.

6. A start-up may obtain crowdfunding through online crowdfunding platforms operated by third parties, or procure crowdfunding themselves.

7. Common types of crowdfunding for business include:

(1) Equity crowdfunding where investors invest in a start-up in return for an interest in shares or debt instruments issued by the start-up, or an interest in participating in the profits or income from the crowdfunding arrangement which is structured as a collective investment scheme.

(2) Peer-to-peer (P2P) lending where the crowdfunding platform matches lenders (investors) with start-ups for providing unsecured loans to the start-ups.

(3) Reward/pre-sale crowdfunding where lenders, instead of an interest or a return in monetary terms can receive physical goods or services from the start-ups in due course.

8. Start-ups often find crowdfunding attractive because it offers relatively easy and less costly access to a wider pool of investors, increases start-ups' visibility in the market and allows start-ups to retain control.

## Relevant Laws and Regulations

## ▌ *No single, specific legislation or regulatory regime*

9. Hong Kong laws and regulations permit and regulate angel investing and crowdfunding. The relevant regulatory requirements are imposed

by various statutes. There is no single, specific legislation or regulatory regime applicable to angel investing or crowdfunding.

10. Accordingly, start-ups should take note of the applicable laws and regulations having regard to the facts and circumstances relevant to them.

## ▌ *Laws and regulations relevant to offer of investments / obtaining funding from investors*

11. CWUMPO[24] contains provisions to the following effects:

(1) A document used by a start-up to offer shares or debentures (which include debenture stock, bonds and any other debt securities) of the start-up to the public amounts to a prospectus and must contain the prescribed contents and comply with the registration requirement under the CWUMPO.

(2) The term "prospectus" is broadly defined in the CWUMPO to include a prospectus, notice, circular, brochure, advertisement or other documents.

(3) The requirements imposed by the CWUMPO on a prospectus are rather onerous. That being the case, start-ups often explore the availability of exemptions or safe harbours to avoid being caught by the requirements, and assess whether they can rely on them in practice having regard to their peculiar facts and circumstances.

(4) The exemptions or safe harbours are set out in the Seventeenth Schedule to the CWUMPO. Subject to compliance with other requirements and conditions imposed by CWUMPO, the ones that may be relevant to start-ups include:

(a) an offer to "professional investors" (which is a term defined under the SFO[25])

(b) an offer to 50 persons or less (i.e. private placement safe harbour)

(c) an offer in respect of which the total consideration payable for the shares or debentures offered does not exceed HK$5,000,000 (i.e. low denomination safe harbour) and

(d) an offer in respect of which the minimum denomination or principal amount or consideration payable by a person is not less than HK$500,000 (i.e. high denomination safe harbour).

12. Section 103 of SFO contains provisions to the effect that:

(1)  It is an offence for a person to issue any advertisement, invitation or document which is or contains an invitation to the public to acquire securities (which include shares or debt instruments issued by a start-up incorporated outside Hong Kong) or participate in a collective investment scheme, unless the issue has been authorized by the SFC or unless an exemption applies.

(2)  However, the SFO has prescribed express exemptions from the Section 103(1) requirement. Whilst these exemptions are to an extent similar to the exemptions or safe harbours prescribed by the CWUMPO, the correlation and interaction between the SFO and the CWUMPO exemptions are not straight-forward. For example, the SFO has prescribed a professional investor exemption but arrangements involving private placement, low denomination investment or high denomination investment are not expressly exempted from the Section 103(1) requirement.

13. Under the SFO, certain types of activities can be viewed as a regulated activity:

(1)  Certain types of activities are defined under the SFO as regulated activities.  It is an offence to carry on business or hold oneself out as carrying on business in regulated activities without being licensed by the SFC for conducting the relevant type of regulated activity.[26]

(2)  If a start-up is considering using crowdfunding platforms or professional services provided by third parties, it should ensure that the relevant third party platform or service providers hold the necessary licences to operate or provide the platforms or services. The licence requirements which may be applicable to these third parties include:

(a)  Type 1 (dealing in securities)

(b)  Type 4 (advising on securities)

(c)  Type 6 (advising on corporate finance)

(d)  Type 9 (asset management)

(3)   The type of regulated activity which is most likely to be directly relevant to start-ups is Type 1 (dealing in securities).

(4)   It is worth-noting that the SFC has only licensed one crowdfunding platform at present for carrying on Type 1 and Type 4 regulated activities.

## ▌ *AML (anti-money laundering) / CTF (counter-terrorist financing) implications and considerations*

14.   Certain funding activities may constitute criminal activities under OSCO[27], DTROP[28] and UNATMO[29]:

(1)   OSCO: it is an offence to deal with any property knowing or having reasonable grounds to believe it to represent proceeds of an indictable offence.[30]

(2)   DTROP: it is an offence to deal with any property knowing or having reasonable grounds to believe it to represent proceeds of drug trafficking. [31]

(3)   UNATMO: A person must not directly or indirectly, deal with any property knowing that, or being reckless as to whether, the property is terrorist property. [32]

(4)   It is important for start-ups to properly verify the source of funds to ensure that they do not fall foul of the above statutes.

15.   It is also worthwhile to take note of AMLO[33] and the following:

(1)   Although the AMLO does not apply directly to start-ups, banks in Hong Kong are subject to the AMLO requirements when handling account opening. Accordingly, start-ups should expect banks to flip the AMLO requirements onto them when processing start-ups' application for opening bank accounts.

(2)   The AMLO imposes various requirements relating to customer due diligence (CDD) and record-keeping on banks, both prior to establishing a business relationship with a customer and thereafter when handling the customer's transactions and account.[34]

(3)   In anticipation of opening a bank account to hold the funding received from angel investors or crowdfunding, a start-up should perform corresponding due diligence and verification of source of funds on its investors.[35]

# ▌ *Latest Development: Public Consultation on Regulation of Crowdfunding Activities*

16. On 19 December 2022, the Financial Services and Treasury Bureau (the "FSTB") published a consultation paper ("Consultation Paper")[36] and launched a 3-month long public consultation on proposals to enhance regulation of crowdfunding activities.

17. As explained by the FSTB, the objective is to build a comprehensive mechanism that can strengthen public confidence to participate in lawful and proper crowdfunding activities (whether online and offline), and prevent lawbreakers from engaging in activities that are fraudulent, jeopardising public interest, or endangering public and national security in the name of crowdfunding.

18. Although there is no indication on the legislative and implementation timeline at this stage, start-ups should stay tuned with the relevant development.

19. Major features of the proposed crowdfunding regulatory regime include the following:

    (1) To set up a Crowdfunding Affairs Office ("CAO") for centrally processing and coordinating regulatory and administrative matters relating to crowdfunding activities, and monitoring the conduct of these activities so that (a) a person is required to make an application to the CAO before conducting a crowdfunding activity that raises funds from individuals or entities of Hong Kong, or from individuals or entities located in Hong Kong, irrespective of whether the person conducting the crowdfunding activity in or from outside of Hong Kong (b) an applicant is required to provide information about itself and details about the proposed crowdfunding activity (e.g., objectives and arrangements), and other information as required by the CAO.

    (2) To consider exemptions and streamlined measures to facilitate the timely commencement and smooth operation of crowdfunding activities which are widely recognised by the society or charitable crowdfunding projects.

    (3) To consider whether to establish a registration system for crowdfunding platforms, and the need to evaluate the coverage and operational practicality given that operations of online crowdfunding platforms vary greatly and are often set up outside Hong Kong.

(4) To empower law enforcement agencies to stop unlawful crowdfunding activities and prosecute offenders.

(5) To exclude the application of the proposed crowdfunding regulatory regime to commercial fundraising activities in the market which are already supervised by financial regulators and subject to existing law and regulations.

## Documentation Required

20. The documentation which may be used in relation to fundraising vary from case to case depending on the investment structure and other factors. Some main documents are discussed below for general reference. The negotiation of the legal documents and contracts is very important to a start-up to ensure that the contractual terms reflect the start-up's intentions and needs and protect the rights and interests of the start-up and its founders, existing shareholders and management team. A start-up should consider seeking help from professional advisers as necessary.

21. Some main documents relating to angel investing include:

(1) Pitch deck —— this is a presentation deck containing information such as viable and sustainable business case, business and growth strategies, key team members and employees, proposed fundraising amount, financials, basic company information etc. in order to arouse the interest of potential investors.

(2) Term Sheet —— this may be prepared by a start-up or an angel investor, often before the start of the negotiation process, to set out the key terms of investment such as the amount of investment, how the investment amount will be used, what the angel investor will obtain in return, whether management control will be retained or shared (and how), the ownership of crucial or valuable assets (e.g. intellectual property), etc.

(3) Subscription Agreement / Shareholders Agreement —— this is the main legal contract to be signed by a start-up (and its existing shareholders where appropriate) and an angel investor which governs the relationship between them (including the establishment, maintenance and termination of such relationship). This contract formally sets out the terms of investment, and the rights and obligations of the respective parties.

(4) Articles of Association of the start-up company ── depending on the investment arrangement, a start-up may need to amend its articles of association or equivalent constitutional document to allow the allotment of shares, the allotment of different classes of shares (if applicable), or (if required by an angel investor) to expressly reflect the rights of an angel investor with respect to various matters (e.g. the right to dividends or returns on its investment, the right to participate in or exercise control over the management of the company, the exit right etc.).

22. Some main documents relating to crowdfunding include:

(1) Pitch deck ── this is a presentation deck containing information such as viable and sustainable business case, business and growth strategies, key team members and employees, proposed fundraising amount, financials, basic company information etc. in order to arouse the interest of potential investors.

(2) Fundraising Agreement / Subscription Agreement / Shareholders Agreement ── this is the main legal contract to be signed by a start-up (and its existing shareholders where appropriate) and its lenders (or the investment vehicle housing the lenders) which governs the relationship between a start-up and its lenders (including the establishment, maintenance and termination of relationship). This contract formally sets out the terms of investment and the rights and obligations of the respective parties.

---

[24] Companies (Winding Up and Miscellaneous Provisions) Ordinance, Cap. 32 Laws of Hong Kong
[25] Securities and Futures Ordinance, Cap. 571 Laws of Hong Kong
[26] Section 114 of the SFO
[27] Organized and Serious Crimes Ordinance, Cap. 455 Laws of Hong Kong
[28] Drug Trafficking (Recovery of Proceeds) Ordinance, Cap. 405 Laws of Hong Kong
[29] United Nations (Anti-Terrorism Measures) Ordinance, Cap. 575 Laws of Hong Kong
[30] Section 25 of the OSCO
[31] Section 25 of the DTROP
[32] Section 8A of the UNATMO
[33] Anti-Money Laundering and Counter-Terrorist Financing Ordinance, Cap.615 Laws of Hong Kong
[34] Schedule 2 of the AMLO
[35] The Anti-Money Laundering and Counter-Terrorist Financing (Amendment) Ordinance 2022 does not change the requirements relating to CDD and record-keeping on banks set out in the AMLO. Accordingly, the obligations of a start-up to take reasonable measures to perform corresponding due diligence and to verify the source of funds on its investors under the AMLO continue to apply.
[36] The Consultation Paper can be accessed at: https://www.fstb.gov.hk/fsb/en/publication/consult/doc/Crowdfunding_consultation_paper_Eng_final.pdf

# Dispute Resolution

## General

1.  The Hong Kong civil justice system offers a range of established processes for the parties to resolve their disputes. Traditional court litigation is only one of the paths available. The alternative modes of dispute resolution are mediation and arbitration. Each of these three options have their own distinct advantages and disadvantages. This Chapter deals with both the traditional and alternative modes of dispute resolution.

## Mediation

2.  Mediation in Hong Kong is an informal, consensual and confidential process that features an impartial mediator. The mediator does not control the outcome of the dispute resolution process. Instead, the role of the mediator is to facilitate the parties in resolving the dispute itself or at least to try to narrow down the parties' differences. It is not essential to involve lawyers in a mediation. Even if lawyers are present to act for the parties, they will play a relatively minor role in the process. Upon reaching settlement in the mediation process, the parties may, depending upon whether or not an action has commenced, either sign a binding settlement agreement or incorporate the terms of settlement in the form of a consent judgment or order based on the terms of settlement. If a party breaches the terms of the settlement agreement, the other party may produce the settlement agreement to a Hong Kong court and ask the court to make an order based on the terms of the settlement agreement reached.

3.  The complete or partial lack of legal representation means that the cost of a mediation is relatively low compared to court litigation and arbitration.  As what was said during the mediation is confidential, the parties are usually more willing to speak freely and may be willing to reveal their bottom line.  The informal environment also means that it is less stressful for the parties and that usually facilitates a more harmonious exchange of views.  If, however, a party has no genuine intention of resolving the dispute and only wants to avoid court litigation or arbitration, the mediation process may be abused and used as a delaying tactic.

4.  In modern day civil disputes, mediation is normally the first step which the parties would take in resolving any form of disputes.  Even if the parties do not go through mediation as a first step, there are court guidelines in Hong Kong which encourages the parties to at least attempt mediation[37].

5.  With the parties' agreement, it is also possible for a Mainland court to conduct mediation[38].  Upon the parties reaching settlement, a Mainland court can issue an official mediation certificate recording the terms of settlement which can be enforced in the same way as a court judgment[39].  Neither party can appeal an official mediation certificate but if a party has evidence to prove that the settlement reached by mediation has violated the principle of voluntariness or the terms of the settlement reached by the parties have been in violation of the law, then such a party can apply for a retrial thereby cancelling the official mediation certificate[40].

## Litigation

6.  If mediation is not successful, the parties will have to resolve their dispute through court litigation unless there is an arbitration agreement made between the parties.  In this regard, the Hong Kong court system has conferred jurisdiction on designated tribunals and courts to resolve virtually all types of disputes depending on the amount claimed and the reliefs sought.

7.  In terms of pure monetary claims, the proper forum for resolving the dispute depends on the amount of the claim:

    (1)  The Small Claims Tribunal[41] deals with monetary claims involving amounts not exceeding HK$75,000.  Legal representation is not allowed and the hearings are usually conducted in Cantonese.

(2)  The District Court[42] deals with pure monetary claims which are more than HK$75,000 but do not exceed HK$3 million as well as non-monetary claims seeking equitable reliefs of small to medium size contracts such as specific performance[43].  Although the parties may appear in person (i.e. appear in Court without legal representation), most of them instruct lawyers to represent them in court as the procedure and the case itself can be quite complicated.

(3)  The Court of First Instance[44] has unlimited jurisdiction and can hear and determine a claim exceeding HK$3 million.

8.    Generally speaking, the processes of the civil proceedings in different courts are similar and may be summarised as follows:

(1)  Pleadings —— The parties are required to set out the factual background of their respective cases in writing.

(2)  Discovery —— Each party is required, as a pre-trial process, to disclose to the other party documents in their possession, custody or power which are relevant to the dispute.

(3)  Witness statements —— The parties may want the court to take into consideration the oral evidence of witnesses when deciding the dispute. This can be done through the preparation of witness statements, the contents of which stand as the parties' evidence in chief in trial and the witnesses can be cross-examined at trial.

(4)  Trial —— Depending on the complexity of the case, the court normally deals with the disputes at trial where lawyers present the case for the parties and witnesses are required to give oral evidence and be cross-examined.  The general public (including the media) is generally allowed to attend the full trial held in an open court as observers.

(5)  Judgment —— After hearing the lawyers acting for the parties and the testimony of the witnesses, the court then rules the dispute in favour of the winning party by way of a reasoned judgment.  The winning party can, generally speaking, claim some of its legal costs from the losing party.

(6)  Appeal —— The losing party may appeal a judgment within the time prescribed by the rules of the court to a higher court.  There are usually two rights of appeal.

9. After judgment is obtained, the winning party may proceed with enforcement (see paragraph 19 below).

10. In the Mainland starting from the lowest with the smallest jurisdiction to the highest with unlimited jurisdiction, there are, broadly speaking, four levels of courts: the district-level People's Court, the municipal Intermediate People's Court, the provincial Higher People's Court and the Supreme People's Court.

11. There are a series of detailed rules governing the geographical and hierarchical jurisdictions of these courts. In a nutshell, most claims for start-ups are probably dealt with in the district-level People's Courts which have jurisdiction to hear and determine a claim of RMB100 million or less and in some instances reaching RMB500 million (in domestic cases) and which have jurisdiction to hear and determine a claim of RMB 20 to 40 million (in foreign-related cases). The losing party may appeal a judgment within the time prescribed by law to a higher court. There is usually only one right of appeal but in special circumstances, an aggrieved party may apply for a review or re-trial of the judgment of the appellate court.

12. In the Mainland, litigation cases are usually heard by a collegiate panel composed of three judges[45]. However, there is available at the district-level People's Court a procedure by which a single judge can hear a case where "the facts are clear-cut, the rights and obligations are straightforward and the dispute is minor", or the parties agree to subject themselves to such a summary procedure[46]. The judgment rendered in a summary procedure involving a claim of a moderate sum (the amount of which varies city to city and ranging from RMB30,000 to RMB70,000) is final and cannot be appealed[47].

13. Chinese is the only official language of court proceedings in the Mainland[48]. All foreign language documents to be submitted to the courts must be translated into Chinese[49].

14. Unlike Hong Kong, there is no "common law style" process for discovery or exchange of witness statements in the Mainland. A party is not required to submit evidence against his or her own interests. Rarely will a Mainland court place much emphasis on the oral evidence of the parties and as such, there is usually no requirement for exchange of witness statements.

# Arbitration

15. When negotiation or mediation is not successful but the parties have entered into an arbitration agreement, the dispute must be referred to arbitration.

16. Arbitration is a consensual and confidential process in which the arbitral tribunal decides the outcome of the dispute. Generally speaking, the parties can agree to appoint one or three arbitrators to form the "arbitral tribunal". The place of arbitration and the rules governing the procedure of arbitration are matters contained in the arbitration agreement. Unlike mediation, arbitration proceedings usually share the features of court proceedings mentioned in paragraphs 8(1) to 8(5) above.

17. After hearing the lawyers acting for the parties and the testimony of the witnesses in the substantive hearing of the arbitration proceedings, the arbitral tribunal then rules the dispute in favour of the winning party by way of an "arbitral award". Subject to a limited number of exceptions[50], an arbitral award is final and cannot be appealed or reviewed. As such, arbitration is usually quicker and cheaper than court litigation.

18. In the Mainland, arbitration is also a popular alternative to litigation for resolving disputes. The process of arbitration in the Mainland is in some ways different from, and generally speaking quicker and cheaper than, that conducted in Hong Kong.

# Enforcement

19. Upon delivery of a judgment or issue of an arbitral award as the case may be, the winning party can enforce the Hong Kong court judgment or the arbitral award (as if it was a court judgment) against the losing party. The important question is whether the losing party has any available assets in Hong Kong. If there are assets available for execution, some common enforcement options include:

    (1) the attachment of funds sitting in the bank account of the losing party or owed by a third party to the losing party as full or partial satisfaction of the judgment debt owed[51]

    (2) the attachment of properties like real estate or shares in a company until full satisfaction of the judgment debt[52]

    (3) the seizure of movable assets of the losing party by the court bailiffs[53]

(4) the winding-up (in the case of a company) or the bankruptcy (in the case of an individual) of the losing party[54].

20. The position is quite similar in the Mainland although the concept of bankrupting an individual is a relatively new one that has been run under a pilot programme in a number of cities including Shenzhen.

21. Subject to a few exceptions, a Hong Kong court generally recognises and enforces a money judgment delivered by a Mainland court which was expressly designated as the court having sole jurisdiction for resolving the dispute in the relevant contract or an arbitral award made in the Mainland pursuant to the PRC Arbitration Law. Similarly, a Mainland court also recognises and generally enforces a money judgment delivered by a Hong Kong court which was expressly designated as the court having sole jurisdiction for resolving the dispute in the relevant contract or an arbitral award made in Hong Kong. The details of the cross border enforcement arrangements are set out in the following documents:

(1) "Arrangement on Reciprocal Recognition and Enforcement of Judgments in Civil and Commercial Matters by the Courts of the Mainland and of the Hong Kong Special Administrative Region Pursuant to Choice of Court Agreements between the Parties Concerned"[55]

(2) "Arrangement Concerning Mutual Enforcement of Arbitral Awards between the Mainland and the Hong Kong Special Administrative Region".

[37] The Rules of the High Court (Cap. 4A), Order 1A rule 4(e)；Practice Direction 31 "Mediation".
[38] Article 96 of the PRC Civil Procedure Law (revised in 2021).
[39] Article 100 of the PRC Civil Procedure Law (revised in 2021).
[40] Article 208 of the PRC Civil Procedure Law (revised in 2021).
[41] Small Claims Tribunal Ordinance (Cap. 338).
[42] District Court Ordinance (Cap. 336).
[43] Proceedings for the specific performance of an agreement for the purchase of a property where the purchase money does not exceed HK$3 million and in case the agreement relates to land, the purchase money does not exceed HK$7 million.
[44] High Court Ordinance (Cap. 4).
[45] Articles 40 and 41 of the PRC Civil Procedure Law (revised in 2021).
[46] Article 160 of the PRC Civil Procedure Law (revised in 2021).
[47] Article 165 of the PRC Civil Procedure Law (revised in 2021).
[48] Article 269 of the PRC Civil Procedure Law (revised in 2021).
[49] Article 73 of the PRC Civil Procedure Law (revised in 2021).
[50] For example, when the parties have expressly agreed by way of prior agreement that an arbitral award can be challenged in Court by reason of "serious irregularity" or on a "question of law".
[51] The Rules of the High Court (Cap. 4A), Order 49.
[52] The Rules of the High Court (Cap. 4A), Order 50.
[53] The Rules of the High Court (Cap. 4A), Order 47.
[54] Companies (Winding Up and Miscellaneous Provisions) Ordinance (Cap. 32)；Bankruptcy Ordinance (Cap. 6).
[55] According to the Department of Justice (https://www.doj.gov.hk/en/mainland_and_macao/RRECCJ.html), this arrangement will be superseded by the "Arrangement on Reciprocal Recognition and Enforcement of Judgments in Civil and Commercial Matters by the Courts of the Mainland and of the Hong Kong Special Administrative Region" signed between the Supreme People's Court and the HKSAR Government on 18 January 2019 upon the enactment of local legislation in Hong Kong. The new arrangement will expand the scope of reciprocal recognition and enforcement of judgments, for instance, to include certain types of non-monetary judgments and replace the condition of sole jurisdiction with other less onerous conditions.

# The Hong Kong Federation of Youth Groups

hkfyg.org.hk | m21.hk

The Hong Kong Federation of Youth Groups (HKFYG) was founded in 1960 and is now the city's largest youth service organisation. For the past six decades, it has been committed to serving the youth of Hong Kong by providing a variety of services, activities and programmes, which have an annual attendance of over six million. We encourage youth to reach their fullest potential, and with community support, we now have over 90 service units. We also have 12 core services, which include the Youth S.P.O.Ts, M21 Multimedia Services, Employment Services, Youth at Risk Services, Counselling Services, Parenting Services, Leadership Training, Volunteer Services, Education Services, Creativity Education and Youth Exchange, Leisure, Cultural and Sports Services, and Research and Publications. Our aim is to motivate young people to grow into responsible and dutiful citizens and we now have over 250,000 registered volunteers and over 500,000 registered members. We believe that our motto **HKFYG • Here for You** reaffirms our commitment and dedication to the young people of Hong Kong.

e·Giving

Online Donation Platform

# About The HKFYG Social Innovation and Youth Business Unit

The HKFYG Social Innovation and Youth Business Unit aims to encourage social innovation by the use of technology. Social problems will also be addressed by innovative and sustainable business models. By engaging young people in the process of social innovation, it makes possible the enhancement of their upward mobility, and makes Hong Kong stay competitive.

## INCUBATION

Providing start-up finding and entrepreneurship training, co-working space, mentorship and training resources to business starters, easing their financial burden.

# YOUTH BUSINESS HONG KONG (YBHK)

From 2005, Youth Business Hong Kong (YBHK) has been supported by donors and foundations to offer one-stop services, including interest-free business loans up to HK$150,000. Since its launch, YBHK has received nearly 2,293 business proposals and 240 were approved, receiving loans amounting to HK$17,424,570.

Fellow entrepreneurs, senior executives in corporations and industry, consultants and other professionals would volunteer their time, expertise and experience as advisors on business operations to support the young entrepreneurs.

## BUSINESS MENTORSHIP

Business Mentorship setting for young entrepreneurs to demonstrate their business profiles, ideas and state their pain points. Groups of experienced and passionate mentors take initiatives to match their strengths with the mentees' pain points, as to provide effective solutions.

## THE HKFYG JOCKEY CLUB SOCIAL INNOVATION CENTRE

Funded by the Hong Kong Jockey Club Charities Trust, The HKFYG Jockey Club Social Innovation Centre was established in 2015. It is located at Genesis, a revitalised industrial building near the Wong Chuk Hang MTR station. SIC occupies nearly 5,000 square feets providing co-working space, business suites, capacity building and incubation programmes for more than 80 start-up companies and 200 young entrepreneurs as of 2023.

QIANHAI SHENZHEN-HONG KONG YOUTH
INNOVATION AND ENTREPRENEUR HUB

## INCUBATION SUPPORT IN GUANGDONG-HONG KONG-MARCO GREATER BAY AREA

The Hong Kong Federation of Youth Groups is one of the initiators of the Qianhai Shenzhen-Hong Kong Youth Innovation and Entrepreneur Hub. We have built connection with different incubation centers in the Greater Bay Area and nominate excellent start-ups for the business development in the Greater Bay Area.

Organized by The Hong Kong Federation of Youth Groups in 2021, the "Supportive Scheme for Young Startup Pioneer in Guangdong-Hong Kong-Macao Greater Bay Area", a "We Venture" project supported by "Funding Scheme for Youth Entrepreneurship in the Guangdong-Hong Kong-Macao Greater Bay Area" under the Youth Development Fund of the Home and Youth Affairs Bureau and the Youth Development Commission, provided 3-year incubation support to 12 successful start-ups . In 2023, 27 partners from 9 Greater Bay Area cites officially signed the strategic cooperation agreement with The Hong Kong Federation of Youth Groups.

# Mayer Brown

Mayer Brown is a distinctively global law firm, uniquely positioned to advise the world's leading companies and financial institutions on their most complex deals and disputes.

With 27 offices and more than 1,800 lawyers in key business centres worldwide, Mayer Brown has extensive reach across four continents. We offer clients in-depth local market knowledge with a truly global reach, which enables us to provide the best solutions for clients wherever their business takes them. Our "one-firm" culture - seamless and integrated across all practices and regions - ensures that our clients receive the best of our knowledge and experience.

Mayer Brown's Hong Kong office is home to one of the largest and longest-established law firms in Hong Kong, supporting local business and serving the broader community since 1863. Conveniently located in Central, our multi-disciplinary team in Hong Kong includes over 60 partners and more than 100 lawyers specialising in various industries, including banking and finance, chemicals, energy, insurance, life sciences, real estate and technology sectors. We provide clients with a full and integrated range of legal services.

With two representative offices in Beijing and Shanghai, we have been supporting our clients in Mainland China since the 1990s. Our solid knowledge of international practice and in-depth understanding of the legal framework governing outbound and foreign investment enable us to leverage the full capabilities of our global firm to connect our legal practitioners with our clients across our worldwide offices.

We provide high-quality legal services in a broad range of practice areas, including:

- Antitrust & Competition
- Banking & Finance
- Capital Markets
- Corporate & Securities
- Cross-Border Mergers & Acquisitions
- Cybersecurity & Data Privacy
- Emerging Companies & Venture Capital
- Employment & Benefits
- Enterprise Risk & Crisis Management
- Financial Services Regulatory & Enforcement
- Global Investigations & White-Collar Defence
- Intellectual Property
- International Trade
- Joint Ventures & Strategic Alliances
- Litigation & Dispute Resolution
- Outsourcing
- Real Estate Markets
- Restructuring
- Tax
- Technology & IP Transactions

Our diverse teams of lawyers are recognized by our clients as strategic partners with deep commercial instincts and a commitment to service excellence.

Community service in Hong Kong is a fundamental part of our firm's heritage. The opportunity to support those in need and the organizations that represent them is one that our lawyers and support staff have enthusiastically sought out over the years. We pursue this through pro bono and corporate social responsibility ("CSR") work, which we believe is a critical component of our profession and an integral part of our true excellence as a law firm.

One of the crucial ways we fulfil our commitment in pro bono work is through supporting education-related programs and organizations. For instance, our lawyers have been partnering with different units of the Hong Kong Federation of Youth Groups. In addition to producing this Legal Guide with their Youth Business

Hong Kong ("YBHK") , our lawyers have been appointed to YBHK's vetting panel to review the business proposals of young entrepreneurs in Hong Kong and in the Greater Bay Area from a legal perspective.

CSR is another channel through which we give back to society and support those in need.   We believe that when the community thrives, we thrive with it. Each year, we tailor our CSR programmes through identifying where we feel we can make an impact for good in the world and immediately around us.  We have participated in activities ranging from clearing up hiking trails and supporting ocean cleaning oyster cultivation to distributing meals to underprivileged communities and mentoring young people with special education needs.  During the pandemic, a number of our colleague stepped up to address the needs of our society through various volunteering initiatives, including distributing anti-epidemic kits across Hong Kong and paying visits to the elderly who lived alone.

Please visit www.mayerbrown.com for more information.

# Contributors

**Mayer Brown**

**Business Vehicles**
Bonnie Yung, Inez Ma, Vanessa Zhou

**Employment**
Jennifer Tam, Vanessa Lo

**Intellectual Property rights**
Michelle Yee, Grace Wong

**Types of Fund Raising**
Evelyn Lok, Sunny Hor

**Social Venture Funding through Angel Investors and Crowdfunding**
Sara Or, Matthew Fok, Bertha Cheung

**Dispute Resolution**
Terence Tung, Raymond Yang, Adrian Law, Huang Xin

**The Hong Kong Federation of Youth Groups**

Gary Tang
May Lee

# Disclaimer

Mayer Brown has collaborated with The Hong Kong Federation of Youth Groups to develop this edition of the Legal Guide. The contents of this Legal Guide are intended to provide general guidance to the subject matters only and should not be construed as legal, accounting, financial or tax or other professional services' advice or opinion. This Legal Guide is not intended to replace specific advice or opinion tailored to individual circumstances and should not be regarded as a substitute for legal or other professional advice from licensed professionals. The authors, editors and publisher of this Legal Guide make no representations or warranties of any kind regarding the accuracy, timeliness, completeness, or applicability of the contents in this Legal Guide, and shall not be held liable or responsible to any individual or entity in any way and for any loss or incidental or consequential damages, howsoever caused by, or arising from the use of, directly or indirectly, the information provided in this Legal Guide. No warranty may be created or extended by any sales representatives or promoters of this Legal Guide or any written sales materials. All risks of loss or damage are solely those of the reader and any liability is hereby expressly disclaimed.

This Legal Guide was prepared on 16 June 2023 and its contents may change at any time due to changes in laws and regulations (and the interpretations of those laws and regulations). Changes in laws and regulations (and interpretations of those laws and regulations) may have significant legal consequences and further, the information provided in this Legal Guide may not be applicable to all companies due to differences in individual circumstances. Readers should seek independent legal advice or other professional advice before taking any action with respect to the matters discussed in this Legal Guide.

Unless otherwise stated, all copyrights and other intellectual property rights in this Legal Guide belong to Mayer Brown and the Hong Kong Federation of Youth Groups. This Legal Guide may be downloaded or printed for personal use or used within an individual company or organization but may only be used for the purpose of personal viewing or for viewing within that company or organization. Any individual or entity is prohibited from reproducing or distributing this Legal Guide to third parties, or using this Legal Guide for commercial purposes, without the prior written consent of Mayer Brown and the Hong Kong Federation of Youth Groups.

## Legal Guide for Business Starters III

| | |
|---|---|
| Publisher | The Hong Kong Federation of Youth |
| Address | Groups |
| | 21/F, The Hong Kong Federation of Youth Groups Building, 21 Pak Fuk Road, North Point, Hong Kong |
| Tel | (852) 3755 7108 |
| Fax | (852) 3755 7155 |
| E-mail | cps@hkfyg.org.hk |
| URL | hkfyg.org.hk |
| Online Bookstore | books.hkfyg.org.hk |
| M21 Youth Portal | M21.hk |
| Edition | July 2023 first edition |
| ISBN | 978-988-76280-8-8 |
| Price | HK$100 |
| Advisor | Andy Ho Wing-cheong |
| Supervisory Team | Ms Helen Hsu |
| Author | Mayer Brown |
| Editorial Board Member | Mr Gary Tang, Ms Miranda Wong |
| Executive Editor | May Lee, Ada Chau, Marco Yu |
| Editorial Intern | Cynthia Liao, Elanie Hui, Eunice Choi |
| Design | Axel C. |
| Printer | Asia One Printing Ltd |

© Copyright 2023
by The Hong Kong Federation of Youth Groups
All rights reserved

青協 APP・立即下載